D0915518

Biographical Sketches of the Delegates from Georgia to the Continental Congress

The Reprint Company
Spartanburg, South Carolina

This Volume Was Reproduced
From An 1891 Edition
In The
University of Georgia Libraries
Athens, Georgia

The Reprint Company
Post Office Box 5401
Spartanburg, South Carolina 29301

Reprinted: 1972
ISBN 0-87152-085-0
Library of Congress Catalog Card Number: 74-187390

Manufactured in the United States of America on long-life paper.

BIOGRAPHICAL SKETCHES

OF THE DELEGATES FROM GEORGIA TO THE CONTINENTAL CONGRESS

BY

CHARLES C. JONES, JR., LL.D.

AUTHOR OF "THE HISTORY OF GEORGIA," "NEGRO MYTHS FROM THE GEORGIA COAST," ETC.

BOSTON AND NEW YORK
HOUGHTON, MIFFLIN AND COMPANY
The Riverside Press, Cambridge
1891

The Riverside Press, Cambridge, Mass., U. S. A.
Printed by H. O. Houghton & Company.

To

THOMAS ADDIS EMMET, M. D., LL. D.,

OF NEW YORK CITY,

WHOSE INTELLIGENT, GENEROUS, AND INDEFATIGABLE

RESEARCHES AND ACQUISITIONS

HAVE ACCOMPLISHED SO MUCH IN RESCUING FROM OBLIVION

NAMES AND EVENTS

MEMORABLE IN THE HISTORY OF AMERICA,

These Sketches

ARE CORDIALLY INSCRIBED.

CONTENTS.

PREFACE.

In the retaliatory acts passed by the Royalist Assembly which convened in Savannah in 1780, the following members from Georgia of the Continental Congress were attainted of high treason; their property, real and personal, was vested in the Crown; and they were declared incapable of holding or exercising any office of trust, honor, or profit: —

"John Houstoun, Rebel Governor.
Lachlan McIntosh, Rebel General.
George Walton, Member of Rebel Congress.
Joseph Clay, Rebel Paymaster-General.
N. Wymberley Jones, Speaker of Rebel Assembly.
Edward Telfair, Member of Rebel Congress.
Richard Howley, Rebel Governor.
William Few, Rebel Counselor.
Edward Langworthy, Rebel Delegate.
Joseph Wood, Member of the Rebel Congress.
Benjamin Andrew, President of the Rebel Council.
Nathan Brownson, Member of Rebel Congress.
Lyman Hall, Member of the Rebel Congress.
Joseph Habersham, Rebel Colonel.
John Habersham, Rebel Major.
William Gibbons, the elder, Rebel Counselor.
Samuel Stirk, Rebel Secretary."

Eight more there are — most of them subsequently elected — whose names do not appear upon this black list. This legislation had been provoked by, and was in retaliation for, an act passed on the 1st of March, 1778, by the Republican General Assembly of Georgia, by the terms of which various parties who clave to the fortunes of the Crown were attainted of high treason, their property, both real and personal, was confiscated to the State, and boards of commissioners were appointed for the purpose of selling their estates and covering the proceeds into the public treasury.

Behold the fearful condition of affairs then dominant in Georgia! Royalists and Republicans contending for the mastery, not only with arms, but each by solemn legislation denouncing the other as traitors, and declaring private property a spoil to that government which could first lay hands upon it! Surely no darker picture was ever painted in the history of civil wars, the most bloody and unrelenting of all strifes. The devastating tread of contending armies — pushed backwards and forwards over the face of a smitten country, crushing the life out of habitations and filling the land with marks of desolation and the scars of battle — is terrible; but far more severe is that fratricidal conflict which disrupts the ties of blood, unseats mercy, dethrones humanity, abolishes the right to private property, and gives the region over to general confiscation, plunder, and murder. Other States there were within whose borders were heard, during the progress of the Revolution, the thunders of broader battles, but truly none can be named in which the calamities of a divided government and the horrors of internecine dissensions were more pronounced.

At that epoch of distraction and peril, there was a deal of courage and sacrifice involved in accepting the position of member from Georgia of the Continental Congress.

Of all the English Provinces in America, Georgia had least cause to revolt against the Mother Country. Since her settlement, that Colony had received, by grant of Parliament, nearly £200,000, besides generous bounties lavished in aid of silk-culture and agricultural products, and various private benefactions. This fact weighed with no little force upon the minds of many; and Governor Wright sought every opportunity to inculcate gratitude towards a government whose paternal interest had been so kindly manifested. For years he presided over the Province with impartiality, wisdom, and firmness. Through his watchful care the Colony had been delivered from the horrors of Indian warfare and guided into the paths of peace and plenty. By his negotiations millions of acres were added to the public domain. Diligent in the discharge of his official duties, strong in his resolves, just in the exercise of his powers, loyal in his opinions, courteous in his intercourse, thrifty in the conduct of his private affairs, and exhibiting the operations of a vigorous and well-balanced judgment, he secured the respect and the affection of his people. Although differing from many of the inhabitants upon the political questions which were then dividing the public mind, he never suffered himself to be betrayed into acts of violence or of revenge. He preferred to counsel, to enlighten, and to exhort. It excites no surprise, therefore, that his influence — vigorously exerted in encouraging loyalty to his royal master and submission to the acts of Parliament — should have had great weight in retarding the progress of rebel thought, and in restraining Georgia, at the outset, from casting her lot with her sister American Colonies, and commissioning delegates through whom she might participate in the adoption of measures which precipitated the war of the Revolution. The apparent tardiness and hesitancy on the part of the Province in joining the Confederation at the inception of those movements which culminated in a declaration of independence may be further excused or accounted for when we remember that she was, of all the original Thirteen Colonies, the youngest and least prepared for the struggle, and when we recall the fact that Schovilites, leagued with Indians, were scourging her borders, and awakening, in the breasts even of the most patriotic and daring, gravest apprehensions for the safety of their wives and children. In the language of Captain McCall, "The charge of inactivity vanishes when the sword and hatchet are held over the heads of the actors to compel them to lie still."

While the record of the services of the members from Georgia in the Continental Congress may not be as brilliant or as valuable as that of some of the Delegates from other Colonies (with the exception of the Reverend Doctor Zubly, and possibly of General Gunn, who never took his seat), they were all good and true men, capable and most earnest in the support of the common cause. Many of them were gentlemen of high culture, superior education, and attractive social and political virtues. Fourteen of them, in one capacity or another, bore arms in the struggle for independence; ten were members of the legal profession; six were merchants; three were physicians; one was a clergyman; and not less than ten were interested in agricultural operations. Engraved portraits have been made of Abraham Baldwin, Archibald Bulloch, Joseph Clay, William Few, Button Gwinnett, John Habersham, Joseph Habersham, Lyman Hall, Noble Wymberley Jones, Lachlan McIntosh, and George Walton. Of the others, so far as we can discover, no likenesses exist.

After the lapse of so many years, and in the absence

of recorded memories, it is difficult, nay impossible, to present as full and accurate sketches as we would wish. Having, however, utilized all the materials at command, we commit this manuscript to the printer in the hope that what we have attempted for Georgia may be better accomplished by others in behalf of the remaining commonwealths associated in the brave and patriotic Confederation of "The Original Thirteen."

AUGUSTA, GEORGIA, 1891.

BIOGRAPHICAL SKETCHES.

BENJAMIN ANDREW.

Born in Dorchester, South Carolina, about 1730, Mr. Andrew led the life of a planter. He came of that sturdy Puritan congregation which, abandoning England in 1630, after a residence of some sixty-five years in Massachusetts, removed to South Carolina and formed a settlement on the northeast bank of the Ashley River about eighteen miles above Charles Town. In 1754 Mr. Andrew, bringing his family with him, left Dorchester in South Carolina, and made a new home in the Midway District, subsequently constituting a part of St. John's Parish in the Colony of Georgia. Here he became the owner of a swamp plantation and engaged in the cultivation of rice.

In the preliminary discussions and demonstrations which eventuated in a declaration of independence on the part of the parish of St. John and afterwards of the Colony of Georgia, Mr. Andrew allied himself with the revolutionists, and, in company with Lyman Hall, Button Gwinnett, Daniel Roberts, Samuel Stevens, Joseph Wood, Daniel Baker, and other local patriots, was earnest in the support of the rights of the American provinces in their struggle with Great Britain for liberation from kingly rule.

In the spring of 1773 William Bartram, the naturalist, who, at the request of Dr. Fothergill, of London, had undertaken a visit to the Floridas "for the discovery of rare and useful productions of nature, chiefly in the vegetable kingdom," gives us this glimpse of the home of Mr. Andrew, then not many miles distant from Midway Meeting House in St. John's Parish. "In the evening," writes Mr. Bartram, "I arrived at the seat of the Hon. B. Andrew's, Esq , who received and entertained me in every respect as a worthy gentleman would a stranger, that is, with hearty welcome, plain but plentiful board, free conversation, and liberality of sentiment. I spent the evening very agreeably, and the day following (for I was not permitted to depart sooner) I viewed with pleasure this gentleman's exemplary improvements in agriculture, particularly in the growth of rice, and in his machines for shelling that valuable grain, which stands in the water almost from the time it is sown until within a few days before it is reaped, when they draw off the water by sluices, which ripens it all at once; and when the heads, or panicles, are dry ripe, it is reaped, and left standing in the field in small ricks until the straw is quite dry, when it is hauled and stacked in the barnyard. The machines for cleaning the rice are worked by the force of water. They stand on the great reservoir which contains the waters that flood the rice-fields below.

"Towards the evening we made a little party at fishing. We chose a shaded retreat in a beautiful grove of magnolias, myrtles, and sweet bay trees, which were left standing on the bank of a fine creek, that from this place took a slow serpentine course through the plantation. We presently took some fish, one kind of which is very beautiful; they call it the red-belly. It is as large as a man's hand, nearly oval and thin, being compressed on each side; the tail is beautifully formed; the top of the head and back of an olive green, besprinkled with russet specks; the sides of a sea-green, inclining to azure, insensibly blended with the olive above, and beneath lightens to a silvery white or pearl color, elegantly powdered with specks of the finest green, russet, and gold; the belly is of a bright scarlet red, or vermilion, darting up rays or fiery streaks into the pearl on each side; the ultimate angle of the branchiostega extends backwards with a long spatula, ending with a round or oval particoloured spot representing the eye in the long feathers of a peacock's train, verged round with a thin flame-coloured membrane, and appears like a brilliant ruby fixed on the side of the fish; the eyes are large, encircled with a fiery iris; they are a voracious fish, and are easily caught with a suitable bait.

"The next morning I took leave of this worthy family, and sat off for the settlements on the Alatamaha, still pursuing the high road for Fort Barrington, till towards noon, when I turned off to the left, following the road to Darian, a settlement on the river twenty miles lower down and near the coast." [1]

We offer no apology for making this quotation, because it conveys a pleasant impression of person and place. Of the first Executive Council convened upon the election of John Adam Treutlen as governor of Georgia in 1777, Benjamin Andrew was chosen president, with Samuel Stirk as clerk. Three years afterwards Mr. Andrew was elected a member of the Con-

[1] *Travels through North and South Carolina, Georgia, etc., etc.*, by William Bartram, pp. 11, 12. London, 1792.

tinental Congress. His associates were Edward Telfair, George Walton, Lyman Hall, and William Few. Upon the conclusion of the war of the Revolution Mr. Andrew became an associate justice for the county of Liberty, and in that capacity sat for several terms with Chief Justice Walton.

One of his sons bore arms in the primal contest for freedom, and subsequently removed from Liberty County to Washington, Wilkes County, where, on the 3d of May, 1794, a son was born unto him, — James Osgood Andrew by name, — who acquired some prominence as a Bishop of the Methodist Episcopal Church, South. The honorable Benjamin Andrew died in Liberty County, Georgia, toward the close of the last century.

ABRAHAM BALDWIN.

When his brother-in-law, the poet Joel Barlow, in speaking of the subject of this sketch, remarked that "the annals of our country have rarely been adorned with a character more venerable, or a life more useful than that of Abraham Baldwin," he indulged in no flattery, but uttered a well merited compliment. Of all the members from Georgia of the Continental Congress, none may be named more scholarly in his attainments, more conscientious in the discharge of duty, more observant of the obligations of the hour, or more useful in the aims and scope of his labors. His chosen way of life lay not across the "weltering field of the tombless dead." On the contrary, his path to preferment was dignified by a dispassionate consideration of grave political problems, — by a calm ascertainment and vindication of the constitutional rights of individuals, states, and nation, — by statesmanlike presentation of the true theory of republicanism in America, and by the promulgation and maintenance of schemes which aimed at the promotion of universal justice, the sustentation of liberty, the higher education of the masses, and the elevation and the happiness of his fellow-man. His mission was exalted, and to its accomplishment he brought a pure heart, — chastened by the influence of a holy religion, — a mind well stored with the learning of the age, much native ability, and tireless industry. Born in Guilford, Connecticut, on the 6th of November, 1754, his collegiate course was pursued at Yale College, whence he graduated in 1772. From 1775 to 1779 he held a tutor's position in that institution. During the last three years of this term, however, and until the close of the revolutionary war he served in the field in the capacity of a chaplain. Upon the consummation of peace, abandoning the clerical profession, he became a student of law. It was upon the recommendation of General Nathanael Greene that Mr. Baldwin removed from Connecticut and acquired citizenship in Georgia early in 1784. Shortly after his arrival in Savannah he was there called to the Bar. Three months afterwards, he was elected a member of the Georgia Legislature, where he originated the plan of the University of Georgia, drew its charter, secured from the State an endowment of forty thousand acres of land, and indicated the catholic lines along which that valuable institution of learning has ever since moved. From the preamble to this charter which, as a whole, has evoked encomiums from the learned and the virtuous, we make the following extract as illustrating the wisdom and patriotism of Mr. Baldwin: "As it is the distinguishing happiness of free governments that civil order should be the result of choice and not of necessity, and the common wishes of the people become the laws of the land, their public prosperity and even existence very much depend upon suitably forming the minds and morals of their citizens. When the minds of the people in general are viciously disposed and unprincipled, and their conduct disorderly, a free government will be attended with greater confusions and evils more horrid than the wild, uncultivated state of nature. It can only be happy when the public principles and opinions are properly directed, and their manners regulated. This is an influence beyond the reach of laws and punishments, and can be claimed only by religion and education. It should therefore be among the first objects of those who wish well to the national prosperity to encourage and support the principles of religion and morality, and early to place the youth under the forming hand of society, that by instruction they may be moulded to the love of virtue and good order. Sending them abroad to other countries for their education will not answer these purposes, is too humiliating an acknowledgment of the ignorance or inferiority of our own, and will always be the cause of so great foreign attachments that upon principles of policy it is inadmissible."

The State of Georgia was then in a most impoverished condition. The losses and distractions experienced during the war just ended had been immense. In the face of every retarding circumstance Mr. Baldwin compassed this important measure; and the University of Georgia is to-day a living monument of his wisdom, prescience, and patriotism. The munificence of the Hon. John Milledge, and the coöperative aid of Governor John Houstoun and the honorables James Habersham, William Few, Joseph Clay, William Houstoun, and Nathan Brownson, were potent factors in the consummation of this educational scheme, which for a century has proven of incalculable benefit to the commonwealth of Georgia. Had he performed no public duty other than this, Mr. Baldwin's title to the gratitude of succeeding generations would have been unquestioned.

His political advancement was rapid. In 1785 he was elected by the Legislature to a seat in the Continental Congress, and from that time until the day of his death he remained in the public service. When he died, four years of his second term as United States Senator from Georgia had not expired.

Of the convention which, in 1787, framed the Constitution of the United States, he was a very active member. It is stated on good authority that some of the essential clauses of that memorable instrument were formulated by him.

"His manner of conducting business," says the author of the sketch which appears in the fourth volume of "The National Portrait Gallery of Distinguished Americans," "was worthy of the highest commendation; he may have wanted ambition to make himself brilliant, but he never wanted industry to make himself useful. His oratory was simple, forcible, convincing. His maxim of never asserting anything but what he believed to be true could not fail to be useful in carrying conviction to others. Patient of contradiction, and tolerant to the wildest opinions, he could be as indulgent to the errors of judgment in other men as if he had stood the most in need of such indulgence for himself."

Mr. Baldwin was a Federalist. So manly was his course in Congress and in the Senate of the United States, so conservative were his views, so conscientious was his conduct in the discussion of all constitutional questions, and so steadfast his adherence to what he cenceived to be the cardinal principles of government, that he acquired and retained in a wonderful degree the confidence of the party to which he was attached, the respect of those who held different notions with regard to the political questions which then agitated the country, and the approbation of his constituents. Of him it has been truthfully said that he "died with the consciousness of having faithfully and fearlessly filled the measure of his public duties."

In private life he was correct in all his habits, and given to benevolent deeds. Never having married, he expended his accumulations in assisting worthy young men in acquiring an education and in establishing them in business. In this regard his charities were akin to those which so beautified the life of Alexander H. Stephens. Upon the death of his father in 1787, he assumed in large measure the payment of his debts and the maintenance and education of his six orphan children. So far as the record stands, the reputation of Mr. Baldwin for purity of character, honesty of purpose and act, fidelity to trust reposed, and genuine benevolence, is most admirable.

To Connecticut is Georgia greatly indebted for Lyman Hall and Abraham Baldwin. Of their adopted citizenship she is justly proud, and in token of her appreciation of their virtuous lives and useful services, she perpetuates their names by two of her counties.

Mr. Baldwin died in harness as a Senator from Georgia, and at the national capital, on the 4th of March, 1807. His last illness was short, and his remains were interred by the side of his friend and former colleague General James Jackson, whom, just one year before, he had followed to the tomb. Although his funeral occurred two days after the adjournment of Congress, many members remained to testify, by their presence, their personal appreciation of the great loss which had been sustained by State and nation. In 1801, and also in 1802, Mr. Baldwin served as president *pro tempore* of the Senate ; and while in Congress he voted in favor of locating the seat of government on the Potomac.[1]

[1] For a fuller sketch of the Hon. Abraham Baldwin, see volume iv. of *The National Portrait Gallery of Distinguished Americans*. Philadelphia, 1839.

NATHAN BROWNSON.

It was upon the invitation of Dr. John Dunwody that Dr. Brownson became a resident of St. John's Parish in the Province of Georgia, and there entered upon the practice of his profession. We are told that he graduated at Yale College in 1761, and that he received his degree of Doctor of Medicine from some Northern institution; but we are not informed of what colony he was a native. Arriving in St. John's Parish, he purchased a small plantation scarcely two miles distant from the present village of Riceboro, in Liberty County, where he builded a home, and with a few slaves began the cultivation of rice. His reputation in the community as a man of intelligence, of sterling qualities, and of excellent professional attainments, was quickly established. At an early date he manifested a lively interest in public affairs, espousing the patriot cause.

Of the Provincial Congress which assembled in Savannah on the 4th of July, 1775, he was a member accredited from the parish of St. John.

Twice was he honored by Georgia with a seat in the Continental Congress; and on the 16th of August, 1781, he was elected governor of that commonwealth. The political skies were then brightening. Augusta had been rescued from the possession of the enemy, and renewed efforts were being made for the recovery of other portions of the State.

Eight days after his induction into office, Governor Brownson, with the intention of strengthening the manhood of Georgia, issued a proclamation requiring all persons who considered themselves citizens of the commonwealth to return to their homes within specified periods, under penalty of being subjected to the payment of a treble tax to be levied upon all lands owned by them within the limits of the State. Many wanderers were thus recalled, who, having forsaken their plantations in Georgia, had sought refuge in the Carolinas and in Virginia. The salary then allowed the governor was at the rate of £500 per annum.

On the 6th of June, 1782, he was appointed Deputy Purveyor for the Southern Hospitals, and at one time during the war he served in the capacity of surgeon in the Continental army.

In the establishment of the state university he took a lively interest. He was named among the grantees to whom Georgia made cession of forty thousand acres of land for educational purposes, and he was one of the original trustees appointed, in 1785, to promote the establishment of an institution of learning. He was twice Speaker of the House of Representatives, and in 1791 presided over the State Senate. Of the convention which, in 1788, ratified the Constitution of the United States, and of the convention which, in 1789, amended the Constitution of Georgia, he was a member. He was also a commissioner on behalf of the State to superintend the erection of the public buildings at Louisville, in Jefferson County, preparatory to the removal of the seat of government from Augusta to that place.

It will thus be perceived that Dr. Brownson was

honored with many public trusts. In the discharge of them all he was capable and most conscientious. There was scarcely any time when his attention was not directed to the performance of some important duty confided to him by his fellow-citizens.

He died upon his plantation in Liberty County, on the 6th of November, 1796. Among the purest patriots and most useful citizens of this region will he always be numbered. The venerable Major Andrew Maybank, who was personally acquainted with Dr. Brownson, related this anecdote: Mrs. Brownson, while a good and faithful wife, was not always pliable, or prompt in responding to the requests of her husband. On occasions the Doctor has been known, in a playful way, to say to her: "Have a care; if you do not acquiesce in my wish, when I am dead I will come back and plague you." Years after the Doctor's demise, the old lady, — his widow, — as she would brush from her nose some vexatious fly or annoying insect, has been heard to exclaim: "Go away, Doctor Brownson;" and as the persistent fly or pertinacious gnat would return, she would, with emphatic gesture and in decided tone, repeat the injunction: "Go away, I tell you, Doctor Brownson, and stop bothering me."

ARCHIBALD BULLOCH.

Of all the patriots who encountered peril and made strenuous exertion to deliver Georgia from kingly dominion and pave the way for her admission into the sisterhood of the confederated American colonies, no one was more earnest, self-sacrificing, valiant, or influential than the honorable Archibald Bulloch. Of irreproachable character, firm in his convictions, brave of heart, bold in action, wise in counsel, jealous of individual and political rights, and thoroughly identified with the best interests of Savannah and of the province of which it was both the capital and commercial metropolis, at an early stage of the revolutionary proceedings he became an acknowledged leader of the rebels, and was by them rapidly advanced to the highest posts of danger and of honor.

Son of the Reverend James Bulloch of Wilton, Colleton Parish, South Carolina, clergyman and planter, and of Jean Stobo, daughter of the Reverend Archibald Stobo, of South Carolina, Archibald Bulloch was born in Charles Town, South Carolina, in 1730. Upon his early education every attention was bestowed. He was destined for the legal profession, and to that end his studies were shaped. Accompanying his father and family upon their removal to Savannah, Georgia, in 1750, from that time forward his interests and sympathies became identified with the development and prosperity of his adopted home. Called to the Bar soon after attaining his majority, he applied himself with zeal and success to the practice of his profession. He married Mary De Veaux, a daughter of James De Veaux, who, in 1760, was senior judge under the administration of Governor Wright. Judge De Veaux was also a large landowner and a successful rice planter.

In 1768, Mr. Bulloch became a member of the Commons House of Assembly, and was named on the committee to correspond with Dr. Benjamin Franklin, who had been appointed an agent to "represent, solicit, and transact the affairs of the Colony of Georgia in Great Britain," and give him such instructions as might appear necessary.

Of the Commons House of Assembly convened in Savannah in 1772, Mr. Bulloch was chosen Speaker, pending a settlement of the dispute between that body and Governor Habersham touching a recognition of Dr. Noble Wymberley Jones. When, upon an inspection of the Journal, his Excellency ascertained that, in disregard of his second disapproval, the House had a third time elected Dr. Jones as Speaker, and that it was only in consequence of his declining to accept the position that the members made choice of Mr. Bulloch, on the 25th of April he sent in this message: —

"Mr. Speaker and Gentlemen of the Assembly:

"I am extremely sorry to find by your Journals that some very exceptionable minutes are entered. I particularly mean your third choice of Noble Wymberley Jones, Esqr., as your Speaker, upon whom I had, agreeable to his Majesty's express instructions, twice put a negative, and that your choice of your present Speaker *was only in consequence of his declining the chair.* If this minute is to stand upon your Journals I have no choice left but to proceed to an immediate dissolution. I desire, therefore, that you will come to a present and speedy determination to recede from it. If you do, I shall, with the most unfeigned satisfaction, proceed to business, which you cannot but be sensible will be of the highest advantage to the Province. I shall expect your immediate answer to this message, that my conduct may be regulated by it; and shall for that purpose remain in the Council Chamber."

To this plucky communication the House, through its Speaker, promptly responded :—

"May it please your Honour:

"We, his Majesty's most dutiful and loyal subjects — the Commons of Georgia in General Assembly met — are very unhappy to find by your message to us of this day that any Minutes entered on our Journals should be construed by your Honour in a manner so very different from the true intent and design of this House. Conscious we are, Sir, that our third choice of Noble Wymberley Jones, Esqr. as our Speaker was not in the least meant as disrespectful to his Majesty, or to you his representative, nor thereby did we mean to infringe on the just prerogative of the Crown. We have seriously reconsidered that particular minute which seems to have given your Honour so much offence, and cannot perceive wherein it is contrary to the strict mode of Parliamentary proceeding, or repugnant to anything communicated to us by your Honour. We were hopeful that no further impediment would have arisen to retard the urgent business of the public, and still flatter ourselves that we may be permitted to do that justice to our constituents which they have a right to expect from us: and we sincerely assure your Honour that it is our hearty wish and desire to finish the business, by you recommended to us, with all harmony and dispatch. ARCHIBALD BULLOCH, *Speaker.*

Governor Habersham, upon the receipt of this response, summoned the House before him in the Council Chamber, and, after a review of the whole affair, finding that he could neither change the mind of the members nor mould their action in conformity with his wishes, peremptorily dissolved the assembly.

Although Governor Habersham's conduct was approved by the king, the effect produced upon the colony was perplexing and deleterious. The treasury was empty, and no tax-bill had been either digested or passed. Important statutes were expiring by their own limitations, and no new laws had been framed for the orderly conduct and support of the province. The inhabitants generally regarded the dissolution as an arbitrary exercise of imperial power, as a violent suppression of popular preference, as an unjustifiable interference with legislative privilege. From across the sea there came no redress of grievances. At home the shadows multiplied, and the waves of unrest, disquietude, and passion chafed more sullenly then ever against the barriers which the ministry had erected.

In 1773 Mr. Bulloch was appointed a commissioner of "Public Roads," and with all the patriotic calls, movements, and assemblages commencing with the 20th of July, 1774, and leading up to the memorable Provincial Congress which assembled in Savannah on the 4th of July, 1775, he was personally and prominently associated. On the 6th of the previous April he had united with Noble W. Jones and John Houstoun in a letter to the President of the Continental Congress explaining the reasons why they — nominated by a convention composed of only five of the twelve parishes constituting the Province of Georgia — could not properly claim to represent the entire colony, or conscientiously apply for admission as delegates from Georgia to the General Congress.

Of the Provincial Congress of the 4th of July, 1775, in which every parish was represented by intelligent delegates, — fit exponents of the dominant hopes and material interests of the communities from which they came, — Archibald Bulloch was unanimously chosen President. By this Congress Mr. Bulloch, John Houstoun, the Rev. Dr. Zubly, Noble W. Jones, and Dr. Lyman Hall, were selected and commissioned as representatives from Georgia to the Continental Congress.

Having memorialized the General Congress, the governor, the citizens of Georgia, and the king, — having framed a bill of rights and proclaimed the privileges for which they were resolved to contend, — having introduced Georgia into the fold of the confederated provinces, — having enlarged the powers of the Council of Safety and appointed committees of correspondence and of intelligence, — having provided the ways and means for future sessions of Congress, and, above all, having demonstrated the inability of the king's servants to control the province in the present crisis, this assembly — certainly one of the most important ever convened in Georgia — adjourned on the 17th of July, subject to further call up to the 20th of August.

Responding to the trust reposed, Messrs. Bulloch, Houstoun, and Zubly repaired to Philadelphia, and participated in the deliberations of the Continental Congress at an adjourned session held on the 13th of September.

The Provincial Congress which assembled in Savannah on the 20th of January, 1776, perfected its organization two days afterwards by the election of the honorable Archibald Bulloch as president. On the 2d of February, he, John Houstoun, Lyman Hall, Button Gwinnett, and George Walton, were appointed delegates to the Continental Congress. Under the temporary constitution then adopted and promulgated, Mr. Bulloch was chosen "President and Commander-in chief of Georgia," with John Glen as Chief Justice, William Stephens as Attorney-General, and James Jackson as Clerk of Court.

On the first of May, 1776, the Council of Safety thus saluted the first Republican President of Georgia:

"MAY IT PLEASE YOUR EXCELLENCY:

"The long session of the late Congress, together with the season of the year, called particularly for a speedy recess: and the House having adjourned while you were out of town, it becomes more particularly necessary for us to addess your Excellency. All, therefore, with unfeigned cönfidence and regard, beg leave to congratulate not only your Excellency on your appointment to, but your country on your acceptance of, the supreme command in this Province.

"It would be needless and tedious to recount the various and yet multiplying oppressions which have driven the people of this Province to erect that government which they have called upon you to see executed. Suffice it thus to declare that it was only an alternative of anarchy and misery, and, by consequence, the effect of dire necessity. Your Excellency will know that it was the endeavor of the Congress to stop every avenue of vice and oppression, lest the infant virtue of a still more infant Province might, in time, rankle into corruption; and we doubt not that by your Excellency's exertions all the resolutions made or adopted by Congress will be enforced with firmness without any regard to any individual or any set of men; for no government can be said to be established while any part of the community refuses submission to its authority. In the discharge of this arduous and important task your Excellency may rely on our constant and best endeavors to assist and support you."

To this address President Bulloch returned the following response:—

"HONORABLE GENTLEMEN:

"I am much obliged to you for your kind expressions of congratulation on my appointment to the supreme command of this Colony. When I reflect from whence the appointment is derived,— that of the free and uncorrupt suffrages of my fellow-citizens,— it cannot fail to stimulate me to the most vigorous exertions in the discharge of the important duties to which I am called by our Provincial Congress. While I have the advice and assistance of gentlemen of known integrity and abilities, I doubt not but that I shall be enabled to enforce and carry into execution every resolve and law of Congress. And, as far as lies with me, my country may depend I will, with a becoming firmness and the greatest impartiality, always endeavor to cause justice in mercy to be executed."

This confidence was well bestowed. To none more capable could this high trust have been confided. President Bulloch was a tower of strength. His personal and official integrity, his exalted conception of honor, his patriotism, his admirable executive abilities, his honesty of thought and purpose, his sturdy manhood, his unquestioned courage, and his enlarged views of the public good, were invaluable in shaping the conduct, confirming the existence, and maintaining the dignity of the infant commonwealth.

Complying with a custom which had obtained during the terms of service of the royal governors, Colonel McIntosh, — commanding the provincial troops in Savannah, — upon the election of President Bulloch, caused a sentinel to be posted at the door of his residence. To this his Excellency objected, with the remark: "I act for a free people in whom I have the most entire confidence, and I wish to avoid on all occasions the appearance of ostentation." Just prior to entering upon his duties as President and commander-in-chief of Georgia, and when Maitland and Grant had retired after their unsuccessful effort to capture the rice-laden vessels lying in the river opposite the town of Savannah, Mr. Bulloch compassed the following dangerous feat: Governor Wright, the officers of the fleet lying in the mouth of the Savannah River, and the British soldiers were in the habit of going ashore on Tybee Island and utilizing for their comfort and enjoyment the houses there situated. This the Council of Safety determined to prevent in future by destroying those edifices. Accordingly a boat expedition — consisting of riflemen, light infantry, volunteers, and a few Creek Indians, led by Mr. Bulloch — on the 25th of March made a descent upon that island, and burned every house except one in which a sick woman and several children were lying. Two marines from the fleet and a Tory were killed, and one marine and several Tories were captured. Although the *Cherokee*, man-of-war, and an armed sloop kept up an incessant fire, the party — consisting of about one hundred men — sustained no loss, and returned in safety to Savannah, having fully accomplished the prescribed mission.

So tardy were the means of communication when the electric telegraph and conveyance by steam were unknown, that the Declaration of Independence — sanctioned in Philadelphia on the 4th of July, 1776 — was not heard of in Georgia until the 10th of August. On that day an express messenger arrived, and delivered to President Bulloch a copy of that memorable document, accompanied by a letter from John Hancock, president of the Continental Congress. The Provincial Council was at once assembled, and in its hearing President Bulloch read aloud that historic utterance of the delegates of the thirteen united colonies. Profound was the impression created, and rapturously did the assembled councilors hail the elevation of British colonies into the dignity of free and independent states.

This ceremony concluded, the President and Members of Council repaired to the public square, where, in front of the building set apart for the deliberations of the Provincial Assembly, the Declaration of Independence was again read, and this time amid the acclamations of the congregated citizens of Savannah. The grenadier and light infantry companies then fired a general salute, and the following procession was formed: —

> "The Grenadiers in front;
> The Provost Marshal on horseback, with his sword drawn;
> The Secretary, bearing the Declaration;
> His Excellency the President;
> The honorable the Council, and gentlemen attending;
> The Light Infantry;
> The Militia of the Town and District of Savannah;
> And lastly, the Citizens."

In this order all marched to the Liberty Pole, where they were met by the Georgia Battalion. Here the Declaration was read for the third time. At the command of Colonel Lachlan McIntosh, thirteen volleys were fired from the field-pieces, and also from the small arms. Thence the entire concourse proceeded to the battery at the Trustees Garden, where the Declaration was publicly read for the fourth and last time, and a salute was fired from the siege guns posted at that point.

His Excellency, the Members of Council, Colonel McIntosh, many gentlemen, and the militia dined under the cedar trees, and cordially drank to the "prosperity and perpetuity of the United, Free, and Independent States of America."

In the evening the town was illuminated. A funeral procession, — embracing a number of citizens larger than had ever been congregated in the history of Savannah, attended by the grenadier and light infantry companies, the Georgia battalion, and the militia, —

with muffled drums, marched to the front of the court house, where his Majesty George the Third was interred in effigy, and the following burial service, prepared for the occasion, was read with all solemnity: —

"For as much as George the Third, of Great Britain, hath most flagrantly violated his Coronation Oath, and trampled upon the Constitution of our country and the sacred rights of mankind: we, therefore, commit his political existence to the ground — corruption to corruption — tyranny to the grave — and oppression to eternal infamy; in sure and certain hope that he will never obtain a resurrection to rule again over these United States of America. But, my friends and fellow-citizens, let us not be sorry, as men without hope, for TYRANTS that thus depart — rather let us remember America is free and independent; that she is and will be, with the blessing of the Almighty, GREAT among the nations of the earth. Let this encourage us in well doing, to fight for our rights and privileges, for our wives and children, and for all that is near and dear unto us. May God give us his blessing, and let all the people say, AMEN."

With similar joy was the publication of the Declaration welcomed in other parishes.

Now that Georgia had been formally recognized as a State, and as it had been recommended by the Colonial Congress that governments should be provided in the several commonwealths adapted to the exigencies of the new order of affairs, and conducive to the happiness and safety alike of the respective States and of the Confederated Union, President Bulloch issued his proclamation ordering a general election to be held between the 1st and the 10th of September, for the purpose of selecting representatives to meet in convention in Savannah on the first Tuesday in October. He also directed that a circular letter should be addressed to the inhabitants of the parishes and districts of Georgia, congratulating them upon the happy political outlook, reminding them of the important business to be transacted by the convention, and impressing upon them the necessity for selecting delegates of approved patriotism and of the highest character,— men whose friendship to the cause of freedom had been thoroughly proven, and whose political wisdom qualified them to frame the best constitution for the future guidance of the commonwealth.

Another proclamation was issued for the encouragement of the recruiting service within the limits of Georgia. It was based upon a resolution of the Provincial Congress which provided that every one entering the army, who should serve faithfully for a period of three years or until peace was concluded with Great Britain, should be entitled to a bounty of one hundred acres of land. It was further stipulated that if he should perish in defense of his State, his widow or family would be complimented with the land.

President Bulloch was careful in explaining to the Indian nations dwelling upon the borders of Georgia the nature of the dispute between the united colonies and England, and in exhorting them to maintain a friendly correspondence.

It was during his administration that General Charles Lee launched his futile expedition against East Florida.

Responding to the proclamation and the circular letter of President Bulloch, the delegates selected by the various parishes assembled in Savannah on the first

Tuesday in October, 1776. They were men of repute at home. They had been carefully chosen and were not insensible to the weighty obligations resting upon them. So numerous were the subjects claiming the attention of this convention, and so exhaustive were its deliberations, that it was not until the 5th of the following February that satisfactory conclusions were reached, and that the Constitution was promulgated which for twelve years defined and supported the rights of Georgia as an independent State. In shaping its provisions, the wisdom and patriotism, the aid and counsel of the Executive were frequently invoked.

Scarcely had this instrument been published when an alarm was again sounded along the southern frontier of Georgia, and the arms-bearing population was summoned to the field. It being found impossible at all times to convene the Council of Safety with a promptitude requisite for the dispatch of urgent business, President Bulloch was, by resolution of that body adopted on the 22d of February, requested "to take upon himself the whole executive powers of government, calling to his assistance not less than five persons of his own choosing to consult and advise with him on every occasion when a sufficient number of councillors could not be convened to make a board."

Unusual as was this delegation of power, it excited neither jealousy nor unfavorable comment. The times were hazardous, delays dangerous, and decision and quick action were imperatively demanded. The prudence, wisdom, courage, and patriotism of Mr. Bulloch were conspicuous. In him did the people trust with a confidence and a devotion rarely exhibited.

But a little while, however, did he survive to exercise these extensive powers. Before the month of February was ended he died[1] suddenly at his home in Savannah, and the State was filled with mourning. He fell in full armor, his thoughts intent upon duty, his arm nerved for the loftiest endeavor. No one of his generation was more influential in shaping the political destinies of Georgia, or more potent in compassing the liberation of that colony from the dominion of the Crown. His good name and patriotic efforts are indissolubly associated with the proudest triumphs of the period. In slight acknowledgment of his services in the cause of freedom and in maintenance of the rights of man, a county has been named in his honor, and he is gratefully remembered as the first Republican President of the commonwealth.

[1] His will was executed on the 11th of February, 1775, and was probated on the 1st of March, 1786. It remains of record in the office of the Ordinary of Chatham County.

JOSEPH CLAY.

Ralph Clay — the father of the subject of this sketch — married Elizabeth, a sister of the honorable James Habersham, intimate friend of the reverend George Whitefield, and, during the absence of Sir James Wright in 1771–72, the royal governor of Georgia. Joseph Clay, the only son of this marriage, was born at Beverley, Yorkshire, England, on the 16th of October, 1741. At the suggestion of his distinguished uncle, supplemented by the persuasions of the Reverend Mr. Whitefield, young Clay came to Georgia in 1760. A few years afterwards, responding to the wish of Governor Habersham, who furnished the means requisite for the adventure, his son James Habersham junior and his nephew Joseph Clay associated themselves in a general commission business in Savannah. The partnership thus formed lasted about five years. With the exception of the period covered by the war of the Revolution Mr. Clay remained actively engaged in commercial pursuits. He and Colonel Joseph Habersham were at one time associated under the firm name of Joseph Clay & Company. He was also a partner in the house of Seth John Cuthbert & Company; at another time he was the senior member of the firm of Clay, Telfair & Company, and again was interested as a copartner in the house of William Fox & Company of Newport, Rhode Island. His home was always in Savannah, where, on the 2d of January, 1763, he married Ann

Legardère. Soon after establishing himself in business in Savannah, Mr. Clay became interested, in connection with his relatives, the Habershams, in the cultivation of rice, which was then the principal market crop produced upon the marish lands of Southern Georgia. Both as a merchant and as a planter he prospered. In conducting his business affairs he was prompt, energetic, and competent.

By the meeting of patriotic citizens assembled at the Liberty Pole at Tondee's Tavern in Savannah on the 27th of July, 1774, he was chosen a member of the committee then raised and charged with the preparation of resolutions expressive of the rebel sentiments of the community, and of the determination of Georgia, at an early day, to associate herself with her sister American colonies in opposition to the enforcement of the unjustifiable and arbitrary acts of the British Parliament.

On the 10th of the following August he appeared with this committee and united in submitting a report which, unanimously adopted, proclaimed in brave language the rights claimed by the protesting provinces, condemned in emphatic terms the policy inaugurated by England, and promised coöperation on the part of Georgia in all constitutional measures devised to obtain a redress of existing grievances and to maintain the inestimable blessings granted by God and guaranteed by a constitution founded upon reason and justice. He was also of the committee then appointed to solicit and forward supplies for the relief of the suffering poor of Boston. In the rape of six hundred pounds of powder from the king's magazine in Savannah during the night of the 11th of May, 1775, and in its subsequent distribution among parties intent upon rebellion, Mr. Clay personally participated. By the assembly convened on the 22d of June in the same year he was complimented with a place in the Council of Safety. To the famous Provincial Congress which met in Savannah twelve days afterwards, he was a delegate accredited from the town and district of Savannah. By that Congress he was placed upon a committee to frame an address to his Excellency Governor Wright. He was also designated as a member of the important "Committee of Intelligence," and commissioned as one of another committee to present the "Article of Association," then adopted, to the inhabitants of the town and district of Savannah for signature.

Deeming it essential to the success of the liberty cause that no officer of the militia should be retained in commission who refused or neglected to sign this "Article of Association," and yet exhibiting a show of respect for Sir James Wright, the royal governor, George Walton, William Le Conte, Francis Harris, William Young, George Houstoun, William Ewen, John Glen, Samuel Elbert, Basil Cowper, and Joseph Clay, acting in behalf of the Council of Safety, on the 8th of August, 1775, addressed a communication to his Excellency the governor, asking permission that the several militia companies of the province should be permitted to elect their own officers. It was suggested that some of them were distasteful to those whom they were appointed to command. Deeming it an extraordinary application, dangerous in its tendency and calculated to wrest the control of the military from the crown officers, Sir James sought the advice of his Council. An answer was returned: "that for many very substantial reasons the governor would not comply with the request." Nothing daunted, the members of the Council of Safety, who really cared but little for the mind of the governor on the subject, took the matter in their own hands, and proceeded to purge the militia of any loyal element which lurked in the ranks of its commissioned officers. The revolutionists were in earnest. With rapid strides they marched forward, overcoming in succession every obstacle which retarded their progress towards the consummation of the complete overthrow of kingly dominion in Georgia. In this rebel procession Joseph Clay was an active and efficient lieutenant.

When, early in March, 1776, Barclay and Grant threatened Savannah, the Council of Safety resolved to defend that town and the rice-laden vessels lying at its wharves, to the last extremity. Mr. Clay was then named as chairman of a committee to inventory and value the shipping in port, and all houses in Savannah and its hamlets belonging to the friends of America who were prepared to participate in the common defense. In that inventory and appraisement were to be included the homes and property of widows and orphans. So firm was the resolution of the patriots, that they were determined to commit everything to the flames rather than have their town and shipping pass into the hands of British soldiers.

The inventory and appraisement were made with a view to future indemnification at the hands of the general government. Fortunately the contemplated sacrifice was not demanded at the hands of these gallant defenders.

On the 6th of August, 1777, Mr. Clay was recognized by the Continental Congress as Deputy Paymaster-General in Georgia, with the rank of colonel. This position was subsequently enlarged so as to embrace the Southern Department. When General Greene assumed command of this department, Colonel Clay was brought into personal association with him, and secured his confidence and esteem. Large sums of money were disbursed by him in the execution of his office, and there remains no suggestion of default or misappropriation. During the years 1778, 1779, and 1780 Georgia named him as one of her delegates to the Continental Congress.

By the first general assembly which convened in Savannah after its evacuation by General Alured Clarke and the king's forces in July, 1782, Colonel Clay was elected Treasurer of the State of Georgia, and his salary was fixed at £300 per annum.

In 1785 he was named as one of the trustees for establishing the college or seminary of learning which subsequently developed into the present University of Georgia; and during the following year he became one of the justices of Chatham County. In May, 1791, he was a member of the committee which welcomed President Washington on the occasion of his visit to Savannah. He died in that city on the 15th of November, 1804.[1]

His son Joseph was a prominent lawyer, and for several years occupied the bench as United States Judge for the District of Georgia. Resigning this

[1] Appleton's *Cyclopædia of American Biography* fixes the date of Colonel Clay's death as the 16th of January, 1805. The true date, as taken from the family records, is that which we have given above.

position he entered the sacred ministry, and was regarded as one of the most eloquent pulpit orators of his day. In later generations the descendants of Colonel Clay have been noted in the church, at the Bar, in the domain of politics, and in social life.

WILLIAM FEW.

Unassisted by family or fortune, yet sustained by natural capabilities, a strong character, a determined will, and a laudable ambition, the subject of this sketch, triumphing over the lack of early education and the retarding influences of the *res angusta domi*, bore a prominent part alike in the Revolutionary annals of Georgia, and in those acts and deliberations which culminated in the establishment of this general government. Brave of heart, firm in purpose, full of patriotic impulse, bred in the school of the self-reliant pioneer, possessing an admirable knowledge of men and events, and exhibiting on all occasions a sound and comprehensive judgment, his counsel and aid were invaluable during the trying epoch when the government of an infant State, changing its seat as the tide of revolution ebbed and flowed in the presence or absence of the king's soldiers, stood in sore need of the substantial encouragement of those accustomed to deal with emergencies and difficulties, and who were loyal to the cause of independence. Material was the assistance rendered by Colonel Few, not only in the shock of arms wherein he took rank with Twiggs, Clarke, Dooly, Elbert, Walton, and Baker, keeping the flame of resistance alive when the territory of Georgia was well-nigh overrun by British regulars, Tories, and subsidized Indians, but also in devising means for sustaining the Revolutionists when they sadly needed arms, clothing, food, organization, munitions, and all sorts of equipments. Potent was his voice in the discussions which eventuated in framing a constitution and in the enactment of laws suitable for the governance of a new State just emerged from kingly rule.

As a Representative from Georgia in the Continental Congress, his course in the national councils was marked by integrity, fidelity, and ability. The reputation acquired at home was here broadened and heightened until it became national in its scope. As a Judge, his conduct was at all times impartial and dignified, and his administration of the law, just, capable, and inflexible. More than once was he called upon to aid in settling the boundary lines of Georgia, and in the pacification of the Indian tribes cormorant near her borders. As one of the original trustees of the state university, his services in devising a scheme for the liberal education of the youths of the land are well remembered. His labors in the convention for revising the Articles of Confederation, and his exertions in behalf of Georgia and her sister colonies in their contest for an independent national existence, were rewarded by a seat in the Senate of the United States. Thus, as a partisan officer, as a member of the Executive Council of Georgia, as a State Legislator, as a Judge, a Trustee, a Commissioner, a Member of Congress, and as a United States Senator, he was complimented with nearly every prominent office within the gift of his adopted State. At all times and in every place did he endear himself to his people; and the value of his patriotic and public services was thoroughly recognized. Faithful and energetic in the hour of doubt and peril, he lived to behold the full triumph of the republic, and to share liberally in the general honors.

Upon his removal to New York in 1799, his services were speedily invoked in the interest of the good order of the community, and the remainder of his life was there spent in usefulness, in the efficient administration of various noted charities, in the discharge of duties appertaining to offices of trust and honor within the gift of the city, and in the proper guidance of the affairs of one of its most respectable financial institutions.

A descendant of one of the early settlers of Pennsylvania, Colonel William Few was born in Baltimore County, Maryland, on the 8th of June, 1748. Removing with his parents to North Carolina when just ten years of age, his boyhood and early manhood were spent in a region where privation and severe labor were the heritage of the many, where opportunities for acquiring even the rudiments of an education were very limited, and where the battle with nature for subsistence and reasonable comfort was incessant and all-absorbing. Even under such disadvantageous circumstances, the longings of his active mind for culture and knowledge were extraordinary, and the progress made in intellectual improvement was quite astonishing. The narrative which he has left of his early struggles unfolds a bright example worthy the emulation of ingenuous youth of the succeeding generations whose lots may be cast in rough places. He came to reside in Georgia in the autumn of 1776. Just twenty-eight years of age, full of vigor and enthusiasm, and accustomed to deal with men, he was there accorded a hearty welcome. Those were stirring times, and almost immediately upon his arrival he threw himself with patriotic ardor into the midst of them, taking an active interest in public affairs, which he maintained during his residence of nearly a quarter of a century in that State.

His life was characterized by probity, decision, independence, strength, courage, and devotion to country and duty. Ardent in temperament, yet deliberate in forming his opinions, he adhered with a tenacity worthy of admiration to all projects promotive of good morals and the general welfare. Toward those entertaining opposite political views he was tolerant and courteous. Candor in thought, word, and act was one of his distinguishing traits. As a partisan officer he was enterprising, intrepid, and patient of every fatigue and privation. The success of the Republic he held superior to every other consideration, and to the cause of the Revolutionists he gave, on every occasion, his unswerving allegiance. In the domestic circle he was affectionate, true, and confiding. A staunch believer in the truths of revealed religion, he governed his life in obedience to the established tenets of the Church of Christ. During his declining years he was much given to meditation and repose. Having acquired an ample fortune, it was his pleasure to disburse all surplus income in support of such charities as commended themselves to his philanthropic heart. In person, Colonel Few was tall, erect, slender, and well-proportioned. His regular and finely poised head was indicative of resolution, intellect, and character. His countenance was agreeable, and his eyes were full of expression. In his manners he was grave and dignified, and his deportment was such as to inspire confidence and respect. He died at the residence of Mr. Albert Chrystie, his son-in-law, at Fishkill-on-Hudson, on the 16th of July, 1828, full of years and of honors.[1]

[1] The following is a summary of the more prominent positions filled by Mr. Few during his long, busy, and useful life : —

1777. Member from Richmond County of the Georgia Legislature.

1777. Member of the Executive Council.

1778. Engaged in the Expedition conducted by General Robert Howe and Governor John Houstoun for the subjugation of East Florida.

1778. Elected Surveyor-General of Georgia.

1778. Appointed Commissioner of Confiscated Estates, and Senior Justice for the County of Richmond.

1779. Appointed Lieutenant-Colonel of the Richmond County Militia, and actively employed in the field in resisting the advance of Colonel Campbell upon Augusta, in guarding the frontiers of Georgia, and in resisting the predatory attacks of British, Tories, and Indians.

1779. A Commissioner on the part of Georgia to bring about a pacification of the Creek and Cherokee nations.

1779. Again a member of the General Assembly of Georgia.

1780. A delegate from Georgia to the Continental Congress.

1781. In obedience to the expressed will of the Continental Congress, present in Georgia to assist in the reconstruction of the State government.

1782. A second time a delegate to the Continental Congress.

1783. Again a member of the Georgia Legislature.

1784. Admitted to the Bar in Savannah.

1786. Reëlected to the Continental Congress.

1787. Delegate from Georgia to the Philadelphia Convention for revising the Constitution of the United States.

1788. Member of the Georgia Convention which ratified the Constitution of the United States.

1789. United States Senator from Georgia.

1793. Again a member of the Georgia Legislature.

1796. Appointed Judge of the Second Judicial Circuit of Georgia.

1799. Removed to New York city.

1801–1804. A member of the General Assembly of New York.

1804. Appointed Commissioner of Loans.

1802. Inspector of the New York State Prison.

1813–1814. Alderman of the 8th Ward of the city of New York.

1804–1814. Director of the Manhattan Bank.

1814. President of the City Bank.

He was also, in 1785, one of the original trustees for establishing the University of Georgia; and was named as a grantee in the cession from the State of forty thousand acres of land as a foundation for that seminary of learning.

Mr. Few united with George Walton and Richard Howley in preparing and signing, in Philadelphia, in January, 1781, the tract entitled "Observations upon the Effects of certain late Political Suggestions," in which they — then representing Georgia in the Continental Congress — protest manfully against the adoption of the *uti possidetis* as a probable basis for peace between England and her American Colonies.

WILLIAM GIBBONS.

The honorable Thomas Spalding, then far advanced in years, in 1850 thus narrates his recollections of the subject of this sketch.[1] "Mr. Gibbons was my law instructor. After my own father he was the best friend I ever knew. He was a great lawyer, well read in his profession, which he acquired in Charleston under the direction of a Mr. Parsons, — an Irish gentleman of high grade in the law. The result from his professional labors while I lived with him was three thousand pounds sterling a year. This I knew, as I was his collector and Mrs. Gibbons his treasurer. There was then no bank paper. His note-book was to him of great value, for he had distinctly noted every important case that had occurred during his whole practice, giving the points on which it turned and the opinion of the judge; and as these judges in those times were Judge Walton of Augusta and Judge Houstoun of Savannah, these decisions carried more weight with the jury than the decisions of the King's Bench.

"Mr. Gibbons was not a very fluent speaker. He was very quick in discovering the weak point of his opponent, and his memory was always ready to give the law that bore upon it. His commentary upon the law was in short, in clear, distinct terms, very pointed; and sometimes he indulged in witticisms, which in-

[1] *The Bench and Bar of Georgia*, vol. ii. p. 102. Philadelphia, 1858.

creased as he grew older from his intimate association with Peter Carnes the elder, — the wittiest lawyer I ever have known, and whose wit obscured his profound law knowledge in the eyes of the many. Mr. Gibbons in his nature was very open, frank, and manly, and very determined. This gave him a few warm friends and many bitter enemies.

"It gives me pleasure to state that General James Jackson, — the noblest man with whom it has been my lot to be acquainted, — when I called upon him as governor[1] to give me a letter to Mr. King, our then Minister in London, kept me to dine with him; and he asked me what were Mr. Gibbons's receipts from his profession? I replied: 'Three thousand pounds per annum.' His response was: 'My own were about that amount when I unwisely left my profession for politics. Mr. Gibbons, *as a whole*, was the greatest lawyer in Georgia.' Let me say to you that General Jackson and Mr. Gibbons had exchanged three shots at each other; they were considered the bitterest enemies by the public. A high-minded man feels no enmity."

Mr. Gibbons was a gentleman of large wealth, accumulated, it is believed, by judicious investment of his professional income. It was upon one of his rice plantations, situated not far from "Mulberry Grove" on the Savannah River, and while as the guest of Mr. Gibbons inspecting his growing crop, that General Nathanael Greene, on the 13th of June, 1786, contracted the illness which so speedily terminated his valuable life. His residence in Savannah was noted for its comfort and bountiful hospitality. It was the

[1] This was in 1798.

day of rich brown sherry, Madeira wine, and good brandy.

Upon another of Mr. Gibbons's plantations General Wayne, in June, 1782, met and overcame the famous Indian Chief Guristersigo.

While intent upon the practice of his profession and busied with his private affairs, he was not indifferent to the claims of country or an idle spectator of passing events. His sympathies at the outset were cordially enlisted on the side of the "Sons of Liberty," and his time and services were cheerfully given to furthering the aims of the rebels.

He was one of the party which, during the night of the 11th of May, 1775, broke open the magazine in Savannah and removed therefrom some six hundred pounds of the king's powder, to be exploded not in the honor, but in defiance of his Majesty.

In the Provincial Congress of July, 1775, he appeared as a delegate from the District of Acton, and was a member of the committee raised to acquaint the president of the Continental Congress with the proceedings of the Georgia Congress.

Of the Council of Safety selected on the 11th of the following December he was chosen a member. It was by direction of this council that Governor Wright was arrested and confined. So far as we can learn, Mr. Gibbons never bore arms during the struggle, but he was almost continuously in the civil service of the commonwealth. Of that Executive or Supreme Council which, in July, 1779, was invested with extraordinary powers, he was an active member.

Aside from the distinction of representing Georgia in the Continental Congress,[1] he was complimented in

[1] In 1784-86.

1786 with the position of Associate Justice of the County of Chatham; in the following year with the speakership of the House of Representatives; and in 1789 with the presidency of the constitutional convention. The act of a formal acceptance, by Governor Walton, from Mr. Gibbons of the new Constitution concluded upon by that convention in Augusta on the 6th of May, was announced to the town by a salute of eleven guns.

Mr. Gibbons died in Savannah in 1800. His will bears date the 14th of June, 1799, and was admitted to probate on the 26th of November in the following year. It is now of record in the office of the Ordinary of Chatham County, Georgia.

JAMES GUNN.

Born of humble parentage and in straitened circumstances in Virginia, in 1739, and having acquired such education as was afforded by the common schools in the neighborhood, Mr. Gunn applied himself to the study of the law, and was in due course called to the Bar.

When the united colonies took up arms against the mother country, he espoused the cause of the Revolutionists, and, in his native State, joined the rebel army.

As a captain of dragoons he participated, under General Wayne, in the movement for the relief of Savannah, Georgia, in 1782; and upon the termination of the war selected that town as his home, and there resumed the practice of his profession.

He was fond of military affairs, and, as Colonel of the First Regiment of Chatham County Militia, led a detachment of state troops which succeeded in dispersing a formidable body of runaway slaves, who, having been trained to arms by the British during their occupation of Savannah, upon the cessation of hostilities styling themselves the "King of England's soldiers," and refusing to return to the abodes of their respective owners, formed a fortified encampment on Bear Creek, and from this place of conjectured security sallied forth by night, plundering and burning adjacent plantations on both sides of the Savannah River.

Subsequently he rose to the grade of Brigadier-General of Georgia Militia, and was, by Governor Telfair, summoned to a council of war to devise measures for the protection of the State against the incursions of the Creek Indians.

Of violent temper and inclined to quarrel, shortly after General Greene became a resident of Georgia, General Gunn challenged him for an alleged wrong which he conceived the general had inflicted upon him during the war of the Revolution. At the time of the conjectured injury, General Greene had been Gunn's commanding officer. Declining the meeting, and disavowing all responsibility in the premises, General Greene planted his refusal upon the broad ground that any admission of accountability under the circumstances would prove totally subversive of all military discipline. The whole matter was referred to General Washington, who unhesitatingly justified the course pursued by his favorite lieutenant.

The Georgia Legislature, then in session at Augusta, on the 10th of February, 1787, elected General Gunn as a delegate to the Continental Congress; but it is believed he never took his seat as a member of that body.

Of the first Congress which convened under the Constitution framed by the Convention of 1787, General Gunn was a member. He was also a United States Senator from Georgia, in 1795 and 1796. While holding this high office he became implicated in the Yazoo speculations, involving personal disgrace and impairing the fair fame of the commonwealth which he represented in the Upper House of the National Congress. He was one of the three grantees of *The*

Georgia Company, and exerted his influence to compass a cession of public lands in direct violation of established principles of justice and equity.

Alluding to this scheme to rob the State of Georgia of its western territory, Doctor Stevens observes:[1] —

"The whole State was heaving with excitement. The bribery which had been so openly used by men high in office on the Bench, at the Bar, and in the Senate, and the corruption, intrigue, intimidation, and violence which had been employed to gain over the Legislature to the plans of the speculators constitute a dark page in the political history of Georgia. One of the most zealous advocates of this scheme was James Gunn. This man, who had risen from almost obscurity to power by truckling to the vulgar tastes of the populace, and by some show of military genius, was, at the period of which we write, a Senator of Georgia in Congress, and his presence there was needed to guard the interests of the State. Yet, sacrificing all public considerations to private advantage, he remained in Georgia, repaired to Augusta, and by his influence and efforts, at once overbearing and unscrupulous, became the main manager of this nefarious business. Having secured the passage of the bill, he then repaired to Congress, which he reached only the last day of February, — four days before the constitutional close of the session, — and there sought to carry out his Georgia schemes by involving the general government also in these questionable transactions."

In these efforts he was thwarted by his co-Senator from Georgia, — a gentleman of the sternest probity, jealous of personal and national honor, and of conspic-

[1] *History of Georgia*, vol. ii. p. 478. Philadelphia, 1859.

uous courage, — the honorable James Jackson. It was chiefly through his potent intervention that the *rescinding act* was passed, that the scheme to rob the commonwealth of its valuable western territory was exposed to public apprehension and reprobation, and that the legislative proceedings of Georgia were purged of this flagrant iniquity. Disgrace and disappointment followed hard upon exposure. Senator Gunn died suddenly at Louisville, Jefferson County, Georgia (then the capital of the State), on the 30th of July, 1801.[1] He was one of those who voted for locating the seat of government on the Potomac.

While an active and brave subaltern in the Continental Army, and a man of determination and of considerable force of character, General Gunn was violent, aggressive, addicted to extravagant statement and profane swearing, overbearing, disposed to pander to the lowest prejudices of the populace, unscrupulous in the means employed for the accomplishment of his ambition, vain, boastful, negligent of public duty when intent upon schemes of personal advantage, and intolerant of opposition. The architect of his own fortunes, he builded a reputation quite marked, but in some respects unenviable.

[1] In the *Georgia Gazette* of August 6th, 1801, appears the following notice of his death: "Extract of a Letter from Louisville, dated July 31. General Gunn arrived here last Sunday, and died last night at eleven or twelve o'clock, a very short illness indeed. It is said that his death was greatly owing to a draught of cold water after the taking of medicine; and, what is strange, the doctor and several gentlemen were in the room, and not one observed his death till some time after he expired. He is to be buried this afternoon with the honors of war."

His will was probated in Chatham County, Georgia, on the 10th of May, 1808, and letters testamentary were granted to Sarah Gunn, executrix.

BUTTON GWINNETT.

WITH the exception of the last five or six years, which were rendered somewhat memorable by an active participation in the events connected with the inception and progress of the Revolution in Georgia, and by his tragic death, Button Gwinnett appears to have spent his life in tranquillity and without special mark. Aside from the Constitution adopted by the Georgia Convention in 1777, which is generally supposed to have been, in large measure, the offspring of his thought and political sagacity, we have no monument either of his literary or public effort. He wrote and spoke but seldom, and his signatures are esteemed among the rarest of the Signers of the Declaration of Independence.

His birth in England occurred almost contemporaneously with the planting of the colony of Georgia, at Savannah, by the illustrious Oglethorpe. That his education was not neglected may be accepted as a fact, although it was perhaps not so liberal as to have inclined him to the adoption of one of the learned professions. In early manhood he engaged in mercantile pursuits in Bristol, England. This city, however, in a spirit of adventure, he soon abandoned, and became a resident of Charles-Town, South Carolina. Here, for a season, he resumed his avocation as a merchant; but, erelong, attracted by the growing importance of the younger Province of Georgia, he transferred his hopes and his property to Savannah, its commercial metropolis. There, as early as 1765, we find him established in the business of a general trader. It was a place of limited means, and trifling were the ventures of its most prosperous merchants.

The establishment of a convenient highway connecting the town of Savannah with the Scotch settlement at Darien, on the Alatamaha River, tended largely to the development and the population of the intermediate swamp region, which was very fertile, and well adapted to the cultivation of rice, cotton, corn, indigo, and vegetables and fruits of various sorts. The regulation prohibiting the introduction of negro slaves into the Province of Georgia had been abrogated, and former restrictions upon the alienation of lands had been removed. Thus encouraged, and allured by the agricultural advantages of this portion of the Province, colonists from other plantations flocked in and possessed themselves of the rich deltas of the Great Ogeechee, the Midway, and the North Newport rivers. The accession of the Dorchester congregation — consisting of some three hundred and fifty whites and fifteen hundred negroes — materially enhanced the wealth and increased the population of this Midway District. It contributed to the rising importance of the village of Sunbury, situated upon a bold and beautiful bluff on Midway River, which, overlooking the placid waters of that stream and the intervening low-lying marshes, descries in the distance the green woods of Bermuda Island, the dim outline of the southern point of Ossabaw, and, across the Sound, the white shores of St. Catharine.

4

When the claim of Mary Bosomworth[1] was finally adjusted, this island of St. Catharine, upon which she had fixed her home, was acknowledged to be her individual property. Apparently dissatisfied with his mercantile pursuits, and anxious to avail himself of the attractions offered by the Midway District, fast becoming the most influential parish in the Province, Gwinnett, about 1768, converted his property into money and purchased a portion of this island from Thomas and Mary Bosomworth. Including some cattle, horses, hogs, lumber, and a plantation-boat, the cost of these premises amounted to £5,250. With some negro slaves he there established a plantation and turned his attention to agriculture. Indigo, rice, corn, and lumber were the staple commodities of the region. His residence was in easy access to Sunbury, then the rival of Savannah in population and commercial importance.[2] With Dr. Lyman Hall — the leading physician in the community, and one of the earliest and most influential "Sons of Liberty" in the Province — he contracted a strong personal and political friendship. To this association may probably be referred the active interest which Gwinnett soon manifested in the political fortunes of the Province, then on the eve of a mighty revolution.

His first public service of which we find any mention

[1] Her Indian name was Cowsaponckesa. Claiming to be of royal blood, she was in turn the wife of John Musgrove, Jacob Matthews, and of the Rev. Thomas Bosomworth, at one time chaplain to Oglethorpe's regiment. She had rendered various and valuable services to the colonists.

[2] On the 16th of September, 1768, Mr. Gwinnett was, by Governor James Wright, appointed a commissioner "for regulating the pilotage for the Bar of Saint Catharine and the river Midway in the Parish of Saint John and Province of Georgia." He also held a commission from the crown as a Justice of the Peace for St. John's Parish.

was rendered as a delegate from the Parish of St. John to the Provincial Congress which convened in Savannah on the 20th of January, 1776. By that Congress he was selected, in association with Archibald Bulloch, John Houstoun, Lyman Hall, and George Walton, as a delegate to the Continental Congress. In that national assembly he appeared on the 20th of the following May, and, as one of the members from Georgia, affixed his signature to the Declaration proclaiming the independence of the United Colonies.

On the 30th of August, 1776, Mr. Gwinnett presented to the Council of Safety certified resolutions of the Continental Congress authorizing the enlistment of a regiment of Rangers, horse and foot, — two battalions, two companies of Artillery to garrison the forts at Savannah and Sunbury to be erected at the expense of Georgia, and the construction of four galleys, to be built at the charge of the general government and under the supervision of the Governor of Georgia, — all intended for the defense of that State, and to be placed upon the Continental establishment. In compassing the passage of these resolutions and in carrying them into practical effect he was largely instrumental.

On the 7th of October in the same year he became a member of the Council of Safety, still retaining his position as a delegate to the Continental Congress.

With the framing and passage of the Constitution of 1777, which for twelve years defined and supported the rights of Georgia as an independent State, Button Gwinnett had much to do. In truth, he was regarded as the parent of that instrument; the provisions of which were, in the main, well considered, wise, and adapted to the emergency. Not a few of them have withstood the changes of more than a century. To the present day are their beneficial influences recognized and approved.

Such was the alarming condition of public affairs, and so menacing the attitude assumed by Florida, that a short time before his death Button Gwinnett, Jonathan Bryan, William Bryan, Adam F. Brisbane, and John Bohun Girardeau — members of the Council of Safety — addressed a communication to President Archibald Bulloch, requesting him "to take upon himself the whole executive powers of government, and to call in to his assistance not less than five persons of his own choosing, with whom he might consult and advise on every urgent occasion when a sufficient number of Councillors could not be convened to make a board."

In February, 1777, Archibald Bulloch — the first Republican President and Commander-in-Chief of Georgia; who was a tower of strength to the Revolutionists; whose personal integrity, high sense of honor, patriotism, admirable executive abilities, honesty of thought and purpose, sturdy manhood, unquestioned courage, and comprehensive views of the public good were invaluable in shaping the conduct and maintaining the dignity of the infant commonwealth; who, with ceremonies the most august, had promulgated the Declaration of Independence in Savannah, and in all his acts had commanded the respect, confidence, and devotion of his fellow citizens — passed away suddenly, the lamp of liberty in his hand trimmed and burning, his noble character, exalted impulses, and brave deeds constituting a precious legacy to his people. The infant State was filled with mourning.

By the Council of Safety was Gwinnett, on the 4th of March, 1777, elected President and Commander-in-Chief of Georgia in the place of President Bulloch. In that capacity he was to serve until such time as a governor could be duly appointed in obedience to existing constitutional provisions. Thus had he rapidly attained unto the highest honor within the gift of the commonwealth.

On the same day the Council of Safety (at the urgent suggestion, it is said, of the newly elected President), "in view of the suffering condition of many of the inhabitants of East Florida inclining them to throw themselves on the people of Georgia for protection, and the alarmed condition of the Southern frontier on account of the frequent inroads and depredations of the Floridians," passed an order "requesting President Gwinnett to march into Florida, with a competent force of militia and volunteers, erecting the American standard as he went, and proclaiming protection and security of person and property to all who would take the oath of allegiance to the United States." He was also urged "to cut off all supplies from the garrison of St. Augustine." In his absence upon the contemplated expedition, Jonathan Bryan was chosen to preside over the Council.

The following is the full text of the commission of Button Gwinnett as President and Commander-in-Chief of Georgia: —

"At a Council held at Savannah, in the State of Georgia, the fourth day of March in the year of our Lord one thousand seven hundred and seventy seven, appointed by the Representatives of the People of the State of Georgia aforesaid:

To our trusty and well-beloved BUTTON GWINNETT, *Esquire,* Greeting:

"Whereas it was thought necessary by the Representatives of the people of this State [then Province], in General Congress assembled on the third day of April in the year of our Lord one thousand seven hundred and seventy-six, to appoint proper officers from among themselves or the people at large for the execution of certain powers to them respectively delegated and intrusted:

"And whereas the same People by their Representatives in Congress assembled did, by their special commission, constitute and appoint their trusty and well-beloved Friend, Archibald Bulloch, Esquire, President and Commander-in-Chief of the State aforesaid, giving and granting unto the said Archibald Bulloch such full power and authority as is in the said commission fully and clearly pointed out and set forth:

"And whereas the said Congress did further resolve that in case of the death or inability to act of such their President, so by them appointed, that then and in such case, during the recess of Congress aforesaid, the Council aforesaid should have full power and authority to appoint from among themselves such other person to the office of President, so happening to be vacant from the causes aforesaid, as to them should seem meet:

"And whereas the said Archibald Bulloch, Esquire, hath since departed this life, whereby the Executive Powers of Administration have devolved upon us the Council aforesaid:

"And whereas we have under those circumstances, in the name of the good People of the State aforesaid, and agreeable to the power vested in us, thought proper to elect and appoint you, the said Button Gwinnett, President and Commander-in-Chief of the said State:

"Know ye therefore that we, the Council aforesaid, during the Recess of the Legislative Body of the State aforesaid, by whatsoever name they may be called, reposing special Trust and confidence in the Prudence, Courage, Patriotism, and Integrity of you the said Button Gwinnett, have thought fit to constitute and appoint, and by these Presents do constitute and appoint you, the said Button Gwinnett, to be *President and Commander-in-Chief of the State of Georgia* aforesaid, agreeable to the powers and authority vested in us by the Resolves and Regulations of the said Congress. And we do hereby charge and command you to do and execute all things in due manner that shall belong unto your said command, and the trust we have reposed in you, according to the several powers and authorities granted or appointed you by this present commission, and the Rules, Laws, and Regulations herewith given you, or by such further Powers, Jurisdiction, and Authorities as shall at any time hereafter be granted or appointed you by the present or any future Legislature of the said State, and according to such Resolves, Laws, and Statutes as now are in force, or hereafter shall be made and agreed upon by any future Legislature of the said State, legally convened under your government, in such manner and form as is hereafter expressed.

"And our pleasure is that you, the said Button Gwinnett, after the publication of this our Commission and Authority, do in the first place take the oath appointed to be taken as President and Commander-in-Chief of the State of Georgia aforesaid: And also take, subscribe, and acknowledge the Test or Declaration also appointed to be taken, subscribed, and acknowledged by the said Congress, which said oath our Attorney General, in the name of us the Council aforesaid, hath full power and authority to administer unto you: And we do hereby give and grant unto you full Power and Authority, with the Advice, Consent, and Approbation of us, the said Council, [whereof seven shall be a quorum] from time to time, as need shall require, to summon and call the General Congress of this State, or by whatever name the same be called, when the same shall be adjourned or any recess thereof happen and necessity require. And you, the said Button Gwinnett, with the Advice and Consent of the Council aforesaid, shall appoint Magistrates to act during pleasure in the several Parishes of this State for the better advancement of Justice, and for the good order and quiet of the people under your command, and putting the Laws in execution, and to administer or cause to be administered unto them such oath or oaths as are now given for the due Execution and Performance of offices and places, and for the clearing of Truth in all cases whatever. And we do hereby authorize, and give and grant unto you full power and authority, with the Advice, Consent, Direction, and Approbation of us, the Council aforesaid, when you shall see cause, or shall judge any offender or offenders in criminal matters who have been found guilty and condemned by the Courts of Justice, properly erected, or for any fines or forfeitures due unto the State, fit objects of mercy, to pardon all such offenders, and to remit all such fines and forfeitures [wilful murder only excepted], in which case you shall likewise have power, upon extraordinary occasions, to grant Reprieves unto the offenders until you may be further advised in the premises. And we do by these presents give and grant unto you, the said Button Gwinnett, with the advice and consent of the Council, by yourself, or by your Captain and Commander by you to be authorized, full power and authority to levy, arm, muster, command and employ all persons whatsoever residing within the said State of Georgia under your Government; and, as occasion shall serve, to march from one place to another, or to embark them for the resisting and withstanding of all enemies, pirates, and powers coming with hostile intention against the State both at sea and land, if necessity shall require for defence of the same against the invasion or attempts of any of our enemies; and such enemies, if there shall be occasion, to pursue and prosecute in or out of the limits of this State: and, if it shall so please God, them to vanquish, apprehend, and take; and being taken, either according to law to put to death, or keep and preserve alive at your discretion.

"And we do hereby give and grant unto you full power and authority, by and with the advice and consent of us, the said Council, to erect, raise, and build in the said State of Georgia, during the adjournment or recess of the said Congress or Legislative Body, such and so many Forts, Platforms, Castles, and Fortifications as you, by the advice aforesaid, shall judge necessary: and the same or any of them to fortify and furnish with ordnance, ammunition, and all sorts of stores fit and necessary for the security and defence of the said State; and by the advice aforesaid, the same again to demolish or dismantle as may be most convenient. And generally to do and execute all and every thing and things agreeable to the laws, regulations, and proceedings of Congress, and the Constitution under which you are called forth to act, and which to you, the said Button Gwinnett — as our President and Commander-in-Chief — doth, or ought of right to belong.

"And we do hereby require, charge, and command all officers and ministers, civil and military, and all other inhabitants of the State of Georgia to be obedient: aiding and assisting you, the said Button Gwinnett, in the execution of this our commission, and of the Powers and Authorities herein contained, and according to the true sense and meaning thereof.

"This commission to continue and be in force until revoked by the Legislative authority of this State.

"Signed and sealed by us in the Council Chamber in Savannah the fourth day of March in the year of our Lord one thousand seven hundred and seventy seven.

JONA[TH] BRYAN.
JA[S]. DUNWODY.
WILLIAM BRYAN.
SAMUEL SALTUS.
B. ANDREW.
ADAM BRISBANE.
JN[O]. B. GIRARDEAU.

By command.

JAMES WHITEFIELD, *Secretary*."

Prior to issuing this commission a resolution had

been adopted by the General Assembly to add three battalions of infantry and a squadron of dragoons to the Georgia troops serving on the Continental establishment, and to form them into a brigade. Colonel Lachlan McIntosh was promoted to the rank of brigadier-general, and assigned to the command of these forces. Gwinnett had been a candidate for this position, and he became thoroughly embittered by McIntosh's success. When he assumed the reins of government he permitted not his anger to slumber. In order to mortify the military pride of his adversary and to impair his influence, he impressed upon the public mind the danger of investing army officers and courts-martial with powers which could possibly be withheld from them and entrusted to the civil authorities. Acting upon this theory, he intervened in military matters to such an extent that he seriously impaired the discipline of the troops, and incited among the officers a spirit of insubordination toward the commanding general. Thus, when an officer was charged with an offense, either civil or military, Gwinnett claimed the right of trying him before the Executive Council. If detailed for special duty, or assigned to a temporary command of moment, he insisted that he should take his orders from the president and council. The effect of all this, as may well be imagined, was demoralizing to the army and most galling to General McIntosh.

Anxious to signalize his administration by a feat of arms, Gwinnett, acting upon the suggestion of Council, planned the expedition against East Florida. The prospect of retaliation was pleasing to the public, and in the breast of the president there lurked an ambitious hope that he would be able to overrun and subdue that sparsely populated province and annex it to Georgia. Instead of entrusting its command to General McIntosh, who, as the ranking military officer of the State, was clearly entitled to expect and to claim it, Gwinnett, heaping affront upon affront, set him aside, and determined in person to lead the expedition. His deliberate purpose was, with the militia of the State and the Continental troops then stationed in Georgia, to form an army of invasion without consulting General McIntosh on the subject, or even allowing him to accompany his brigade. The movement was to be immediate. Proclamations were printed which he proposed to scatter broadcast through the land so soon as he crossed the river St. Mary. He labored under the impression that, to insure success and encourage the inhabitants to a change of government, nothing would be needed save to hoist the standard of liberty in Florida and make a show of a supporting army. Advised, however, that the province of East Florida was in large measure peopled by loyalists from Georgia and South Carolina, that no reliance for subsistence could be placed upon the products of the region, and that an accumulation of supplies was requisite before he could venture upon the expedition, he abandoned his scheme as at first chimerically entertained.

Still intent upon the consummation of his ambitious project, and reiterating his resolution to lead the army in person, he assembled his Council, denominating it for the time being a *council of war*, and concerted the following plan of operations. Sawpit Bluff, twelve miles from the mouth of the river St. John, was designated as the place, and the 12th of May as the time, for the rendezvous of the forces which were to participate in the contemplated reduction of East Florida. Colonel Baker, with the Georgia militia, was to march by land, while Colonel Elbert, embarking four hundred of the Continental troops in three galleys and several small boats, was to repair by water to the point indicated. Having, with great difficulty, crossed the Alatamaha River at Fort Howe, Colonel Baker moved with only one hundred and nine men in the execution of the order entrusted to him. Near Nassau River he was defeated by Colonels Brown and McGirth, and his command was wholly dissipated.

Colonel Elbert was sorely perplexed upon finding that he was commissioned to lead the Continental forces, detailed for the expedition, to the exclusion of General McIntosh, who, as his superior officer, was entitled to claim that distinction. He was also greatly concerned at the abnormal condition of affairs brought about by orders emanating from President Gwinnett and his Council, by which he was required to report directly to, and to receive his instructions from, the Governor and Council. Communicating with General McIntosh, he advised him of the disagreeable situation in which he found himself, and expressed his regrets that the orders issued did not come through him as his commanding general. He even went so far as to remonstrate with the Governor and Council in regard to this irregularity. Gwinnett, however, controlled his Council, insisted upon his rights as commander-in-chief, and, being of an imperious will and implacable in his hate, continued to supplant General McIntosh and to subject him to humiliation. The detachment of Continentals led by Colonel Elbert utterly failed in its purpose; and so, without benefit and pregnant with disaster, ended an expedition conceived in ambition and jealousy, planned without due caution, and sadly marred in its execution.

Responding to the emergency caused by the lamented death of Archibald Bulloch, and in the exercise of his gubernatorial powers, President Gwinnett issued a proclamation requiring the several counties of the State to elect delegates to a legislature which should convene in Savannah on the first Tuesday in May, 1777. The first and chief duty of this assembly was to elect a successor to President Bulloch. Gwinnett was an avowed candidate for the position. The Legislature met in due season, and, after organizing by the selection of Dr. Noble W. Jones as speaker and Samuel Stirk as secretary, proceeded to the choice of a governor. John Adam Treutlen was elected by a handsome majority. Grievous was Gwinnett's disappointment. McIntosh did not hesitate to openly avow his gratification at the result. In fact, he publicly and in the presence of the members of the Executive Council denounced Gwinnett as a scoundrel. The quarrel between these gentlemen culminated on the 15th of May, when Gwinnett challenged McIntosh to mortal combat. The challenge was promptly accepted. They met the next morning at a spot within the present limits of the city of Savannah. Pistol shots were exchanged at the short distance of four paces. Both were wounded in the thigh: McIntosh dangerously, Gwinnett mortally. The former was confined to his couch for some time, and the latter, after lingering for four days, died of his hurt.[1]

[1] For Dr. Lyman Hall's account of this duel, see his sketch, *post*.

Intense excitement ensued. Dr. Lyman Hall, one of Gwinnett's executors and a warm personal friend of the deceased, and Mr. Joseph Wood brought the matter to the notice of the Legislature, and charged the judicial officers with a neglect of duty in not arresting McIntosh and binding him over to answer an indictment for murder. Informed of these proceedings, so soon as his wound permitted, the general surrendered himself to Judge Glen and entered into bonds for his appearance. He was indicted, tried, and acquitted. Even this determination of the matter did not allay the malevolent feelings of the Gwinnett party, who, incensed at the loss of their leader, used every exertion to impair the influence of McIntosh and to fetter his efforts in the public service. Moved by these untoward circumstances, and yielding to the suggestion of his friends, the general consented to leave Georgia for the time being, and repaired to General Washington's headquarters for assignment to duty with the Continental army. Nearly two years elapsed before he returned to the State. During that time he rendered valuable service in the common cause.

The tradition lingers that Button Gwinnett was interred in the old cemetery in Savannah. So far as our information extends, no stone marks his grave, and the precise spot of his sepulture has faded from the recollection of succeeding generations. When the monument which rises in front of the City Hall in Augusta, perpetuating the memory of the signers from Georgia of the Declaration of Independence, was erected, the hope of its patriotic builders was that it would cover the dust of all three of them. The mortal remains of Dr. Lyman Hall and of Chief Justice George Walton were readily found, and were then committed to the guardian care of this memorial shaft. After careful search, no trace could be discovered of the last resting-place of Gwinnett, and he still sleeps in a grave which will probably never be identified.

Specimens of the chirography of this signer are very rare. He evidently wrote but little. He died in the forty-fifth year of his age, and his public life extended through only a few years. We have looked upon his original will. It still exists. It is a holograph. The following is a literal copy of it:—

SAVANNAH, *March* 15th, 1777.

Im sound in Body and Mind for which I am under the highest obligations to the Supreme Being. How long I shall remain so God only knoweth: I therefore Dispose of my Property[1] both real and Personal in the Following manner.

First. Let all my Just Debts be Discharged, then One half of my Real and Personal Estate remaining be divided between my Wife and Daughter in equal Shares.——

The other Half of my Estate both real and Personal shall belong to and appertain unto the Revd Mr Thos Bosomworth his Heirs and Assigns forever, he the said Thos Bosomworth first giving a rec^{t} in full of all other Demands.——

This is my last Will and Testament and I hereby revoke all other Wills and Codicils.

The above is only intended to convey my Estate in America.

[1] Besides his plantation on St. Catharine Island, Mr. Gwinnett was the owner of Sutherland's Bluff,—a tract of a thousand acres of land in Liberty County,— and of several other parcels of well-located land.

I hereby appoint Thos Savage and Lyman Hall Esqr^{s} as Executors to this my last Will and Testament.

BUTTON GWINNETT [seal].

Witness
Ja^{s} Foley.
Wm Hornby.
Thom^{s} Hovenden.

The foregoing will was admitted to probate by James Whitefield, "Register of Probates," on the 30th of May, 1777. On the same day Lyman Hall qualified as Executor.[1]

It would appear by the affidavits of William Hornby and Thomas Hovenden, — two of the subscribing witnesses, — that while this will bears date on the 15th of March, 1777, it was actually published and witnessed on or about the 16th of May, 1777. Hornby's affidavit reads as follows: —

Christ Church Parish & County of Chatham } Court of Registry of Probates.

William Hornby of Savannah & State aforesaid Gentl^{n} personally appeared & being sworn maketh Oath that the within named Button Gwinnett Esqr did, on or about friday the 16th day of this inst May, deliver the paper to this deponent, now produced, purporting to be his will, and said to this deponent in words following, vizt "this is my Will, sign as a witness thereto, and keep it, and if anything happens to me read it & you'l know what to do with it;" and this deponent further saith He verily believes He, the said Button Gwinnett, the Testator, was, at that time of

[1] The inventory and appraisement of the estate of Mr. Gwinnett are on file in the office of the Ordinary of Chatham County, Georgia.

5

sound and disposing mind and memory; and that at the time He signed the same as a witness, He saw Ja^{s} Foley's name also subscribed thereto as a witness, & further saith not.

WM. HORNBY.

Sworn the 30th
May 1777 Before
Jam^{s} Whitefield
Reg^{r} of Probates.

Thomas Hovenden, in his affidavit, corroborates the statement made by Mr. Hornby. We extract the following from his oath made before the Register of Probates on the 30th of May, 1777: "The within named Button Gwinnett Esqr dec^{d} did, on or about the 16th day of this ins^{t} May, deliver the paper now produced, in his presence, to Mr Wm Hornby, a subscribing Witness thereto, saying at the same time 'that it was His Will,' or words to that purpose, and asked this deponent to sign the same; and this deponent says that He did sign his Name thereto as a Witness, & further saith that He is well acquainted with the Hand writing of the said Button Gwinnett Esqr dec^{d}, and that he verily believes that the said paper now produced as his will is in the Hand writing of the said Button Gwinnett," etc.

The period was hazardous, and life peculiarly uncertain. We conclude that Gwinnett drew his will at the time the instrument bears date in anticipation of leading his projected expedition against East Florida, and then signed it, but failed to have it witnessed. In this state the instrument remained in his hands until, warned by the impending duel with McIntosh, and upon the eve of that unfortunate affair, he completed its publication and committed it to the care of Mr. William Hornby, one of the subscribing witnesses, with an injunction which denotes at least some apprehension on his part of the possibility of his encountering a mortal hurt in the approaching combat.

Brief but brilliant was the career of Button Gwinnett. Rising like a meteor, he shot athwart the zenith of the young commonwealth, concentrating the gaze of all, and, in a short moment, was seen no more. Within the compass of a very few years are his brilliant aspirations, triumphs, and reverses compressed. Without the accident of birth or the assistance of fortune, he was advanced, and that most rapidly, to the highest positions within the gift of his countrymen. Inseparably associated is his name with the charter of American independence. Of his intelligence, force of character, ability to command success, courage, indomitable will, tenacity of purpose, patriotism, love of liberty, and devotion to the cause of American freedom, he gave proof most abundant. But he was ambitious, covetous of power, strong in his prejudices, intolerant of opposition, and violent in his hate.

Of this signer we believe no well-authenticated portrait exists. His name dignifies a county in Georgia, but we know of none among the living in this State in whose veins courses a drop of blood inherited from, or kindred with, that of Button Gwinnett.

JOHN HABERSHAM.

THIS gentleman — the third son of the Honorable James Habersham and Mary Bolton — was born on the 23d of December, 1754, at Beverley, the country seat of his father, about nine miles from Savannah, Georgia. He was baptized by the Reverend Bartholomew Zouberbuhler, the rector and incumbent of Christ Church in that city. His preparatory studies having been completed at home, he matriculated at Princeton College, New Jersey. From this institution he graduated with distinction.

Scarcely had he attained unto manhood when he identified himself with the Revolutionists, and was soon numbered among the most zealous advocates of American independence.

On the 7th of January, 1776, he was mustered into continental service as the first lieutenant of the first company of the battalion raised at the charge of the United Colonies for the protection of Georgia. Of this command his brother Joseph was commissioned Major. With three hundred men of that battalion he was present when Colonel Lachlan McIntosh, from the hastily constructed works upon Yamacraw Bluff, armed with three four-pounder iron field-pieces, opened fire upon the British troops led by Maitland and Grant, who were seeking to capture and take to sea the rice-laden vessels congregated at the wharves and along the opposite shore of the Savannah River.

He was shortly afterwards announced as Brigade-Major of the Georgia forces upon the Continental establishment, of which Lachlan McIntosh was the ranking officer and Samuel Elbert the second in command. In this capacity he accompanied the expeditions planned, and launched in succession by General Charles Lee, by President Button Gwinnett, and by General Robert Howe and Governor John Houstoun, for the reduction of St. Augustine and the subjugation of Florida. At Fort Tonyn, where marked dissensions arose between General Robert Howe commanding the Continental troops, Governor Houstoun controlling the Georgia militia, and Commodore Oliver Bowen conducting the supporting fleet, Major Habersham was a member of the council of war which, in view of the distractions existent in the American camp, because of the sickness prevailing in the army, and in consideration of the intervening obstacles, resolved it was imprudent to advance further and attempt the passage of the river St. John. These expeditions were characterized by lack of preparation, mismanagement, disagreement between commanders, surprising mistakes, vexatious delays, and fruitless expenditures of men and munitions. Upon the return of the Georgia Continental troops from Fort Tonyn, Colonel John McIntosh, with one hundred and twenty-seven men, was posted at Sunbury. General Howe repaired to Charleston, South Carolina, and the regiments of Colonels Elbert and White were sent to Savannah.

An anticipated season of rest and comparative inaction was speedily interrupted by the unexpected advance from Florida of two columns, led respectively by Colonels Fuser and Prevost, — the one moving by land and the other transported by water,—both having as their objective the capture of the town of Sunbury, and, in the end, the investment of Savannah.

While Lieutenant-Colonel Mark Prevost's progress was being sharply contested by Colonels Baker and White and by General Screven, Colonel Elbert, with his command, took post at Ogeechee ferry and fortified that crossing, intending there to deliver battle if the English commander succeeded in penetrating to that point. The failure of Colonel Fuser to effect a junction at Sunbury on the expected day, and the stout resistance offered, induced Colonel Prevost to retrace his steps. Treating the population as in open rebellion against a lawful sovereign, and utterly ignoring all rights of the invaded, that officer, upon his retreat, burnt Midway Meeting-House, and all dwellings, negro quarters, rice-barns, and improvements within his reach. The entire region was ruthlessly plundered. The track of the retiring column was marked by smoking ruins. British soldiers and Tories, unrestrained, indulged in indiscriminate pillage, appropriating plate, bedding, wearing apparel, and everything capable of easy transportation. The inhabitants, particularly of St. John's Parish, were subjected to indignities, and were, in many instances, reduced to absolute want.

Acting under a commission from Colonel Elbert, Major Habersham held an interview with Prevost, in which certain stipulations designed to protect the invaded territory from pillage and conflagration were proposed. The English commander, however, declined to give any guaranty in the premises, and insisted that inasmuch as the inhabitants were rebels against the Crown they must abide all consequences, how grievous soever they might be.

After the affair near Midway Meeting-House, in which General Screven was severely wounded, Major Habersham bore a flag to Colonel Prevost, requesting, in the name of Colonel Elbert, permission to furnish the captured general with such medical aid as his dangerous situation demanded. In response, Doctors Braidie and Alexander were permitted to attend upon him; but they found, upon examination, that his wounds were mortal, and that their surgical skill was impotent to prolong his valuable life.

During the successful assault by Colonel Campbell upon the American forces under General Howe, posted to the east and south of Savannah for its protection, on the 29th of December, 1778, Major Habersham, still acting as Brigade-Major to Colonel Elbert who held the left of the line, is said, by Captain Alexander Wylly, to have been entrusted with the service of a part of the rebel artillery. Finding it impossible, in the face of the impetuous charge of the enemy, to withdraw his field-pieces, and, at the supreme moment, ordering his cannoneers to save themselves, he refused to quit his guns until they were completely enveloped by the foe. The story runs that, perceiving personal capture inevitable, he deliberately broke his seal upon one of the cannon to prevent its passing into the ownership of his captors.

When the retreat was sounded a panic ensued, and the Americans made their way, as best they could and in a confused manner, through the town. Before the retiring army gained the head of the causeway traversing Musgrove's swamp west of Savannah, — the only pass by which the retrograde movement could be accomplished, — the enemy secured a position so as to interrupt the crossing. By heroic exertions Colonel Roberts kept the British at bay until the American centre effected its escape. The rebel right wing, being between two fires, suffered severely and was well-nigh annihilated by wounds, death, and capture. The left, under the command of Colonel Elbert, — who always fought to the last, — continued the conflict with such gallantry and pertinacity that escape by the causeway became impracticable. That officer was therefore compelled to lead his troops, after forcing their way through the town, through the rice-fields lying between the causeway and the Savannah River. In doing so he encountered a damaging fire from the enemy, who, pressing forward, had taken possession of the eastern end of the causway and of the adjacent high grounds of Ewensburg. Reaching Musgrove Creek, he found it filled with water, for the tide was high. Consequently only those of his command who could swim succeeded in crossing, and this they did with the loss of their arms and accoutrements. All others were either drowned or captured. Among the latter was Major Habersham. Colonel George Walton, badly wounded, had fallen into the hands of the enemy.

In this disastrous and sadly conducted affair the Americans lost eighty-three killed and wounded. Thirty-eight officers and four hundred and fifteen non-commissioned officers and privates were made captive. Forty-eight pieces of cannon, twenty-three mortars, a considerable quantity of small arms and ammunition, a fort, the shipping in port, and, above all, the capital of Georgia, were among the substantial trophies of this victory. Upon the fall of Savannah, Southern

Georgia quickly passed under the dominion of the king's forces. Rapidly advancing, Colonel Campbell pushed his exultant column as far as Augusta, and even beyond.

The next occasion upon which Major Habersham, whose detention by the enemy does not appear to have been of long duration, was brought face to face with the British was in the battle of Brier Creek, when General Ash was surprised and defeated by Colonel Prevost.

We may not here revive the memories of an engagement which reflected so severely upon the reputation of an American general and inflicted such loss upon rebel arms. It is proper to state, however, that the only ray of light amid the gloom of the whole affair was shed by the gallantry of Colonel Elbert and his command. That officer, assisted by Lieutenant-Colonel John McIntosh and Major John Habersham, with sixty continental troops, one hundred and fifty Georgia militia, and a field-piece, held the left of the line of battle. Although the right and centre quickly broke and fled in wild confusion, he prolonged the conflict until nearly every member of his force was either killed, wounded, or captured. If we are correctly informed, Major Habersham was here, a second time, made prisoner. He was exchanged, however, in season to participate in the siege of Savannah in September and October, 1779, which culminated in the ill-advised, bloody, and futile assault by the allied army under Count D'Estaing and General Lincoln upon the British lines.

The depressing effect upon the king's forces in America produced by the surrender of Lord Cornwallis at Yorktown, the junction of the auxiliary troops under General St. Clair, and the recent successes of General Greene in the Carolinas enabled that officer, in January, 1782, to redeem his promise for the relief of Georgia. General Wayne was detached for that purpose. "To reinstate, as far as might be possible, the authority of the Union within the limits of Georgia" was the mission of the hero of Stony Point.

Ever since Savannah, in December, 1778, passed into the hands of the enemy, it had become a favorite resort of the Creeks and Cherokees. There were deputations from the Indian nations entertained. There were royal presents distributed, and there were concocted schemes for the annoyance of the republicans. Aware of his acquaintance with, and conscious of the influence he was capable of exerting over the natives, knowing that parties of Indians still visited that town, and desirous of either winning them over to the American cause or of inducing them to remain neutral in the pending struggle, General Wayne dispatched Major Habersham to intercept and conciliate them. He was attended by Major Francis Moore, in command of some South Carolina cavalry, and by Captain Patrick Carr, who led a body of mounted militia. At first Major Habersham was successful in his negotiations. His plans were subsequently frustrated by reason of the indiscretion and disobedience of a lieutenant who, with a portion of the mounted militia, slew several of the Indians present, and then, making a rapid descent upon Sunbury, killed eleven loyalists, residents of that town. Matters were further complicated by the conduct of Major Moore, who, learning that the Creek Indians had stolen some horses on the frontier of Liberty County, insisted upon going in pursuit of them. These and similar transactions defeated Habersham's mission, which otherwise might have resulted in accomplishing much good.

So closely was Savannah now invested by the forces under General Wayne, and so desperate grew the situation of the king's soldiers in Georgia, that on the 23d of May, 1782, Sir Guy Carleton issued, at New York, an order for the evacuation both of that town and province. The authorities were notified that transports would be provided for conveying away not only the troops and military stores, but also Governor Wright and all adherents of the Crown who might desire to depart. Although not unanticipated, this announcement created a profound impression alike upon soldiers and civilians within the royal lines. The latter were most anxious to ascertain what their status would be under the changed condition of affairs, and to secure from the republican authorities pledges that they would not be molested either in person or property. Negotiations were accordingly opened, and to Major John Habersham — an officer in the Georgia line, a native of Savannah, a gentleman whose personal character inspired confidence, and whose high-toned sentiment, correct conduct, and polished address commanded the thorough confidence and respect even of those who were inimical to the cause which he espoused — were they confided on the part of the patriots. That they were conducted by him in all fairness and with becoming dignity, intelligence, and fidelity, it seems scarcely necessary to add.

Savannah having been occupied by General Wayne on the 11th of July, 1782, before setting out to rejoin

General Greene, he detailed Lieutenant-Colonel James Jackson with his legion, and Major Habersham with his corps of new recruits, to take charge of that town and vicinage until civil government should be regularly established. So far as Georgia was concerned, the war was practically ended. Following close upon the heels of the military came the members of the Executive Council. The Legislature quickly convened, and entered upon the passage of such laws as were demanded by the emergency and were deemed most conducive to the general good.

By the disqualifying act of July 6, 1780, passed at Savannah by the Royalist Assembly, Major Habersham, in association with other prominent members of the republican party in Georgia, had been declared incapable of holding or exercising any office of trust, honor, or profit. Upon the termination of English rule in Georgia this legislation became utterly void, and the penalties prescribed were subsequently reckoned as tributes to the worth and patriotism of those upon whom they were sought to be inflicted.

As a proof of the public esteem in which he was held he was, in 1784, elected president of the Executive Council. In that capacity he opened the Land Court in Augusta.

During the years 1785 and 1786 he was a member, from Georgia, of the Continental Congress. In October, 1786, as the chairman of the Commissioners appointed for that purpose by the State of Georgia, he held, at Shoulder-Bone Creek, in Hancock County, a congress at which fifty-nine chiefs, head-men, and warriors of the Creek nation were present. The deliberations of that convention resulted in the conclusion of a treaty, which was signed on the 3d of the following November, stipulating for the peaceful conduct of the Indians, and confirming the boundary lines as agreed upon in the former treaties solemnized at Augusta and Galphinton.

Another important service rendered by Major Habersham was that performed by him, as one of the Commissioners from Georgia, in accommodating at Beaufort, South Carolina, in April, 1787, all differences touching the boundary line between those States. The agreement then reached was reduced to the form of a treaty, which was subsequently ratified by the Congress of the United States and also by the General Assembly of Georgia. By the action of this convention a dispute between sister States, which promised to be a source of continued irritation, was amicably and satisfactorily adjusted.

It was a tribute to his reputation as a gentleman of liberal views and of education when, under the provisions of the Act of the General Assembly of the 27th of January, 1785, he was constituted a member of the first Board of Trustees to establish the University of Georgia, and "advance the interests of literature through the State."

In 1789 he was nominated and confirmed as the collector of the port of Savannah. This office he continued to hold until his death, which occurred ten years afterwards. He was summoned hence in the zenith of his usefulness, in the full possession of all his faculties, and at the early age of forty-five. Lanman fixes the date of his demise as the 19th of November, 1799. The writer is assured by his granddaughter — Mrs. William Neyle Habersham — that he breathed his last in the city of Savannah on the 17th of December, 1799, just three days after the lamented demise of General George Washington, and while the land was filled with mourning at the sudden departure of the *Pater Patriæ*.

Major Habersham was in all respects an estimable man, fearless, honest, patriotic, public-spirited, and, in his domestic relations, tender and true. He was the friend of the widow and orphan; and, as adviser and guardian, in many instances rendered gratuitous and most acceptable service. In his official acts, and in the execution of the responsible trusts confided to him, he was upright and efficient. As an officer of the Continental army he was prompt, courageous, and self-sacrificing. To the cause of the Revolutionists, even in its infancy, was his cordial allegiance given, and he never swerved from its support until the independence of the United Colonies was fully established. Upon the organization of the Georgia branch of the Society of the Order of the Cincinnati, he was complimented with the position of its first secretary.

The influence which he exerted over the Creek and Cherokee Indians is said to have been widespread and salutary. If we are correctly informed, General Washington, while President of the United States, secured his good offices as Indian agent for a portion of the Southern Department. Upon closing his accounts with the general government, a balance arose in Major Habersham's favor which remains unpaid to the present day.

The following anecdote is told by a member of his family. On one occasion he entertained, in Savannah, several Indian chiefs. The leading mico of the delegation was "Mad Dog." Upon seating himself at the table, this chief plunged his knife into the joint of beef which was before him, and drew it into his plate. It constituted the *pièce de résistance* of the feast. When informed by his host that it was subject to partition among his companions, the hungry savage reluctantly restored it to the dish, and sulked until the meal was concluded. A suit of clothes, however, presented by the Major, restored his equanimity and confirmed his friendship.

The old cemetery on South Broad Street in Savannah, wherein sleep so many who were famous and loved in the early days of the colony and commonwealth, guards the dust of this distinguished Georgian; and a beautiful county in the upper portion of the State perpetuates a family name which for nearly a century and a half has been here saluted with gratitude and honor.

JOSEPH HABERSHAM.

He was the second son of the Honorable James Habersham — a native of Yorkshire, England — and of Mary Bolton, and was born in Savannah, Georgia, on the 28th of July, 1751.

Among the worthies who during the colonial period ministered to the intellectual, moral, political, and material development of Georgia, no one is more gratefully remembered than the Honorable James Habersham. The purity of his character, the nobility of his aims and impulses, the utility of his acts, and the influence of his virtuous life were at the time, and have ever since been recognized and admired.

From the date of his arrival in Savannah early in 1738 in company with his friend the Reverend George Whitefield, the famous evangelist and noted philanthropist, until his demise in 1775, he was prominently identified with every movement which contemplated the amelioration of the condition of the Colonists and the promotion of the welfare of the Province. He is specially remembered in connection with the foundation, the control, and the sustentation of the Orphan House at Bethesda; as a most intelligent instructor and guide of youths; as the organizer of the earliest Sunday-schools; as a capable and earnest catechist; as a valued correspondent of the home authorities, keeping them advised of the progress of affairs, and furnishing apt suggestions with regard to the administration of the Trust; as instrumental in procuring a rescission of the regulation prohibiting the introduction of slave labor into Georgia; as a kind and thoughtful master, providing for the temporal wants and the spiritual edification of his numerous servants; as the founder of the earliest mercantile house in Savannah, enjoying high credit both at home and abroad, and possessing commercial relations with Philadelphia, New York, Boston, the West Indies, and England; as the efficient secretary of the Colony; as an energetic commissioner of silk-culture; as an assistant to Mr. Graham, president of the Province upon the surrender, by the Trustees, of its management, and prior to the erection of the royal government; subsequently, as secretary and registrar; and, finally, as the governor *pro tempore* of Georgia during the absence of Sir James Wright.

For this responsible position his education, his personal acquaintance with the inhabitants, his thorough knowledge of the history, development, and wants of the Colony, his long experience in the conduct of its public and domestic affairs, the purity of his character, and the high esteem in which he was held, admirably qualified him. He was the firm friend of law, order, the Established Church, and of the British Constitution. Loyal to his king, his affiliations were with those who obeyed the acts of Parliament, observed the orders of the Lords Commissioners of Trade and Plantations, and maintained their allegiance to the throne of England. In this mind he lived and died. He closed his eyes just as the storm of the primal Revolution began to overshadow the land. While his sons espoused the "patriot cause," their honored father kept faith with his king; and, in departing, lamented the division of

6

political sentiment which was engendering fratricidal strife and betokening a bloody and relentless war.

It excites no surprise that the elder, the wealthier, and the more influential citizens of Georgia should, in the main, at this epoch, have tenaciously clung to the fortunes of the Crown and sincerely deprecated all idea of a separation from the mother country. To such a course were they prompted by natural allegiance, by tradition, and by the strongest ties. Besides all this, of the American colonies Georgia had subsisted most generously upon royal bounty, and had been the recipient of favors far beyond those accorded to sister plantations. The younger members of the leading families, however, in many instances, sympathized with the revolutionists, and thus division arose even within the household. While James Habersham, Noble Jones, the elder Houstoun, the elder Tattnall, and others enjoying distinction in the annals of the Colony, avowed and maintained to the last their devotion to the realm, their sons were found among the earliest and the most potent advocates of a speedy and radical separation from the parent nation.[1]

[1] In an old Family Bible of the Habersham family appears the following entry: "James Habersham, the most respected and lamented Parent of the persons whose births and deaths are recorded in this Sacred Book, was born at Beverley, Yorkshire, England, in the year 1712, and died at Brunswick, New Jersey, 28th August, 1775, aged 63 years. His corpse, attended by two of his sons who were with him at the time of his decease, was carried to New York and interred in a vault of Trinity Church, preparatory to its removal to Savannah, — the funeral service being performed by the Rector of that church.

"On the 14th of November [following] the corpse was landed from the Sloop *Hope*, — Captain Andrew Brown, — and deposited in the family vault in our Cemetery [on South Broad Street, in Savannah, Georgia].

"He was among the early and most useful settlers of the Province of Georgia, and discharged some of the most honorable trusts under the

After a preparatory course of study pursued in the best schools in Savannah, Joseph Habersham repaired to Princeton College, then under the presidency of the famous Doctor Witherspoon, and there completed his collegiate education. While at college he exhibited that quick, ardent temper, that brave and chivalrous spirit, and that independence of thought and action, which so signally characterized him in after life. Returning home he at once and unhesitatingly avowed his sympathies with the "Liberty Boys," and was by them accorded position replete alike with responsibility, with honor, and with danger.

In association with Dr. Noble Wymberley Jones, Edward Telfair, William Gibbons, Joseph Clay, John Milledge, and a few others, — most of them members of the Council of Safety, and all zealous in the cause of American liberty, — at a late hour on the night of the 11th of May, 1775, he broke open the king's magazine in Savannah, and removed therefrom some six hundred pounds of gunpowder; a portion of which, if we may credit a well-approved tradition, was forwarded to Cambridge, Massachusetts, and issued to the rebel army.

As a member of the Council of Safety, he corresponded with the Continental Congress and with other patriotic bodies, and was instant in devising measures for the defense of Georgia and the enkindling of a warlike flame within her borders.

In July, 1775, under the joint leadership of Joseph Habersham and Captain Bowen, a detachment of picked

Royal Government with such unsullied Integrity, Loyalty, and Independence, as to acquire for him the esteem and respect of the wise and the good of our Community.

"He was a sincere Believer in the Christian Religion, and lived up to its precepts as far as the infirmities of our Nature would allow."

men, conveyed in a Georgia armed schooner[1] commissioned by Congress, effected, at the mouth of the Savannah River, the capture of Captain Maitland's ship direct from London and freighted with gunpowder and other military stores. At the earnest solicitation of the Continental Congress, five thousand pounds of this powder were forwarded to Philadelphia, where they were issued to the armies of the United Colonies. From the same source were the magazines of Georgia and South Carolina supplied.

Of the Provincial Congress, which convened in Savannah on the 4th of July, 1775, and placed the Province of Georgia "on the same footing with her sister colonies," he was a leading member; and on the 7th of January in the following year he was appointed major of the battalion raised for the protection of Georgia, of which Lachlan McIntosh was made colonel, and Samuel Elbert lieutenant-colonel. Subsequently, he rose to the rank of colonel in the Continental army.

When the Council of Safety resolved upon the arrest and confinement of Sir James Wright, the royal governor, so that there might be no longer any show of English dominion within the limits of the province, Major Habersham volunteered for and successfully performed the service. Governor Wright was arrested in his residence, which occupied the lot at a later date graced by the home of Governor Telfair. Through the munificence of his daughters, this Telfair mansion has been converted into an academy of arts and sciences.

The bravery of the act cannot be too highly com-

[1] This schooner, armed with "ten carriage guns and many swivels," and carrying a complement of fifty men, is said to have been the first provincial vessel commissioned for naval warfare in the Revolution; and this the first capture made by order of any Congress in America.

mended; and the physical courage displayed was transcended by the moral heroism involved in thus openly defying the power of the Realm, and in humbling the duly constituted representative of the Crown in the presence of the Colony he was commissioned to rule. The effect was startling, — dramatic.

In frustrating the attempt of Captain Barclay and Major Grant to capture the shipping lying in the port of Savannah, during the memorable siege of Savannah in September and October, 1779, and on various occasions during the progress of the War of the Revolution, Colonel Habersham rendered gallant and important service.

The struggle ended, he was twice honored by an election to the Speaker's chair in the General Assembly of his native State. From 1785 to 1786 he was a delegate to the Continental Congress, and in 1788 was a member of the convention which ratified the Federal Constitution. In 1792 he was mayor of the city of Savannah. The year previous he was one of the committee which complimented President Washington with an address of welcome upon the occasion of his visit to Savannah.

By President Washington was he appointed, in 1795, Postmaster-General of the United States. This position he filled with entire acceptability also during the presidential term of the elder Adams. Upon the accession of Mr. Jefferson, he was the recipient of a polite note conveying a tender of the office of Treasurer of the United States. Interpreting this as an intimation that his resignation of the position of Postmaster-General would be agreeable to the newly elected President, he promptly surrendered his portfolio[1] and returned to Savannah, where, entering upon a mercantile life, he essayed to repair a fortune which had been seriously dissipated by the calamities of war.[2] In 1802 he became the president of the Branch Bank of the United States at Savannah. This office he retained until his death, which occurred on the 17th of November, 1815.

The commercial house of Harris & Habersham, organized by his father in 1749, was, after the lapse of many years, practically revived by Colonel Habersham. To the present day it has been perpetuated by members of the Habersham family, and at all times with marked probity, influence, and success.

"We have said," remarks another, "that Colonel Habersham was quick and ardent in temper; but,

[1] It is believed that in this removal of Colonel Habersham — indirectly and delicately compassed as it was by Mr. Jefferson — occurred one of the earliest illustrations of the application of the doctrine, "to the victors belong the spoils." His selection by General Washington to fill the office of Postmaster-General of the United States was wholly unsolicited on his part, and must be regarded as a special tribute to the character and ability of Colonel Habersham. "At a period when so many, from great and devoted service to the country, had claims to office, and these claims well known and appreciated, and when the selection was made by Washington, this appointment was the best evidence of his great merit and of the general estimation in which he was held. In this office, as has been already stated, he continued until the accession of Mr. Jefferson to the presidency. But he retained the office so long by no cringing or truckling to the higher authorities; for the President, Mr. Adams, having told him that the post-office department was an Augean stable, and must be cleansed, — meaning that the postmasters who were of the opposite party must be removed, — Colonel Habersham replied that these officers had discharged their duty faithfully, and that therefore *he* would not remove them, but that the President could remove the Postmaster-General. This, however, Mr. Adams, it seems, did not think proper to do." *National Portrait Gallery*, vol. iv., article, "Joseph Habersham."

[2] He was a member of the commercial house of Joseph Clay & Company.

although quick to take offense, he was ready and anxious to make atonement for the slightest wrong; kind and indulgent to his slaves; humane and liberal to the poor; strict in the performance of all his contracts; tenacious of his own as he had been of the rights of his country. Allowing to others the same independent and frank expression of opinion which he always exercised for himself, he may with truth be pronounced to have been a fine specimen of that noble, generous, and chivalric race which achieved the liberty and independence of our happy country.

LYMAN HALL.

THE subject of this sketch was a descendant in the fifth generation of John Hall, who, coming from Coventry, England, crossed the Atlantic in the ship Griffin, and, after a sojourn in Boston and New Haven, established his home at Wallingford, Connecticut. In this village Lyman Hall, son of the Hon. John Hall and Mary Street, was born on the 12th of April, 1724.

Graduating from Yale College in 1747, in a class of twenty-eight members, several of whom attained distinction in after life, he entered upon the study of theology under the guidance of his uncle, Rev. Samuel Hall. His purpose undergoing a change he abandoned the idea of becoming a minister of the gospel, and applied himself to the acquisition of a medical education. After quite a thorough preliminary course he was admitted to the degree of Doctor of Medicine, married Mary Osborne, and commenced the practice of his profession in his native town.

Early in 1697 a body of Puritans from the towns of Dorchester, Roxbury, and Milton, in Massachusetts, taking with them their pastor, Rev. Joseph Lord, and proclaiming their desire to encourage the foundation of churches and the promotion of religion in the Southern planations, removed with their families and personal effects and formed a new residence at Dorchester, on the left bank of the Ashley River, not many miles above Charlestown in South Carolina. Here these enterprising colonists multiplied in numbers and increased in wealth, exerting a strong moral and political influence. Attracted by tidings of the prosperity of this settlement, and anxious to advance his professional and personal interests, Dr. Hall — himself in full sympathy with the religious tenets of these Congregationalists — in the twenty-eighth year of his age abandoned his home at Wallingford, and cast his lot among the Puritan dwellers at Dorchester and Beach Hill in South Carolina. He was cordially welcomed, and appears at once to have secured the confidence of the community.

After a residence of rather more than fifty years in this swamp region of Carolina, finding their lands impoverished and insufficient for the rising generation, Dorchester and Beach Hill proving unhealthy, — the good reports of the lands in southern Georgia having been confirmed upon the personal inspection of certain members of the society who had been sent for that purpose, and a grant[1] of 22,400 acres of rich land having been secured from the Georgia authorities, — the members of the Dorchester society, in 1752, began moving into what is now the swamp region of Liberty County. This territory lay between Mount Hope Swamp on the north and Bull Town Swamp on the south. Begun in 1752, the immigration continued until 1771, and embraced about three hundred and fifty whites and fifteen hundred negro slaves. The influx of this population was most marked during the years 1754, 1755, and 1756. It was about this time that Dr. Hall, following the fortunes of his newly formed friends, accompanied them to the Midway settlement,

[1] This grant was subsequently enlarged by the addition of 9,950 acres.

and became the owner of a small plantation a few miles north of Midway Meeting-House on the line of the Savannah and Darien highway, — a road connecting the northern and southern confines of the province, which had been completed under the guidance of Tomo-chi-chi and by the command of General Oglethorpe. The region into which the Dorchester congregation thus immigrated was known as the "Midway district." The country was densely wooded, marish, and filled with game. Ducks and geese in innumerable quantities frequented the low grounds, creeks, and lagoons. Wild turkeys and deer abounded. Bears and beavers dwelt in the swamps, and buffalo herds wandered in the neighborhood. There was no lack of squirrels, raccoons, opossums, rabbits, snipe, woodcock, cranes, herons, and rice-birds. Wildcats and hawks were the pest of the region, while the cry of the cougar was often heard in the depths of the vine-clad woods. The waters were alive with fishes, alligators, terrapins, and snakes.

In utter disregard of the manifest laws of health, these immigrants located their dwellings and plantation quarters on the edges of the swamps, and in such malarial situations passed the entire year. While corn, potatoes, and peas were planted on the upland, chief attention was bestowed upon the cultivation of rice. To that end, the swamps, at great labor, were cleared, ditched, and drained. A miasmatic soil was thus exposed to the action of the sun; and, as a direct consequence of injudicious location and a too frequent inattention to domestic comfort, occurred violent sickness and considerable mortality.

Dr. Hall found ample employment for his best professional skill, and endeared himself to the community by his unremitting exertions to counteract the pernicious influences of bilious fevers during the summer and fall, and pleurisies in the winter and spring.

In 1758 Mark Carr conveyed three hundred acres of land bordering upon Midway River to certain trustees, with instructions to lay out a town to be called Sunbury. So soon as the lots were surveyed and designated, many members of the Midway congregation, attracted by the beauty and salubrity of the location, became purchasers, and there established their summer homes. Among them was Dr. Lyman Hall, who bought two of the most desirable lots, numbers 33 and 34, fronting on the bay. Here he built a residence, and spent most of his time when not actively employed in visiting his patients. His reputation as a successful practitioner and sympathizing friend was most enviable. In fact, he speedily became the leading physician of the town and adjacent country. His polite address, literary attainments, public spirit, social habits, thoughtful views, and well-rounded character united in rendering him popular and influential with the inhabitants of St. John's Parish. That he entertained a lively interest in public affairs, and enjoyed the confidence of his fellow-citizens, is evident from the prominence accorded to him when the differences between England and her American colonies were seriously discussed, and the question of a separation from the mother country was gravely considered. His sympathies from the first were with the "Liberty Boys," and his arguments and labors were boldly expended in compassing liberation from kingly rule. Georgia occupied a position peculiar among her sister colonies. Since her settlement she had received by grant of Parliament nearly £200,000, besides generous bounties extended in aid of silk culture and various agricultural products. The paternal care of the Crown had been kindly and signally manifested in her behalf. As a natural consequence, there existed a marked division of sentiment upon the political questions which agitated the community during the years immediately preceding open rupture between England and America. The royal party was active and strong, and it required no little effort on the part of the rebels to acquire the mastery and place the province fairly within the lists of the revolutionists. The line of demarcation was sometimes so sharply drawn that father was arrayed against son, and brother against brother. Thus, not to multiply examples, the Hon. James Habersham and Colonel Noble Jones maintained their allegiance to the Crown, while their sons were among the foremost champions of the rights claimed by the rebels. The cruel effects of such disagreements, experienced prior to and during the progress of the Revolution, were projected beyond even the final establishment of the republic. Governor Wright was most energetic in upholding the fortunes of his royal master, and succeeded in delaying action on the part of the Colony. Through his influence, Georgia was not represented in the first session of the Continental Congress. The Parish of St. John — which then possessed nearly one third of the aggregate wealth of Georgia, and the citizens of which were noted for their thrift, courage, honesty, and determination — chafed under the inaction of the province, which bred dissatisfaction at home, and called down denunciation most violent from the republican party in South Carolina. The Puritan element in the parish, cherishing and proclaiming intolerance of Established Church and of the divine right of kings, impatient of restraint, accustomed to independent thought and action, and careless of associations which encouraged tender memories of and love for the mother country, asserted its hatreds, its affiliations, and its hopes with no uncertain utterance, and appears to have controlled the action of the entire parish. In commenting upon the disturbed condition of affairs, Governor Wright advised the Earl of Dartmouth that the head of the rebellion in Georgia should be located in St. John's Parish, and that the revolutionary measures there inaugurated were to be mainly referred to the influence of the "descendants of New England people of the Puritan independent sect," who, "retaining a strong tincture of republican or Oliverian principles, have entered into an agreement among themselves to adopt both the resolutions and associations of the Continental Congress."

On the revolutionary altars erected within the Midway district were the fires of resistance to the dominion of England earliest kindled; and of all the patriots of that uncompromising community Lyman Hall, by his counsel, exhortations, and determined spirit, added stoutest fuel to the flames. Between the immigrants from Dorchester and the distressed Bostonians existed not only the ties of a common lineage, but also sympathies born of kindred religious, moral, social, and political education. It is therefore not difficult to perceive why the Midway settlement declared at such an early period and in such an emphatic manner for the revolutionists.

Dissatisfied with the failure of the Savannah Congress to place the province in direct association with the other twelve American colonies, the inhabitants of St. John's Parish, under the leadership of Lyman Hall, resolved "to exert themselves to the utmost, and to make every sacrifice that men impressed with the strongest sense of their rights and liberties, and warm with the most benevolent feelings for their oppressed brethren, can make to stand firmly or fall gloriously in the common cause." They called a convention of their own, extending invitations to the inhabitants of other parishes, in the hope "that, if a majority of the parishes would unite with them, they would send deputies to join the General Congress, and faithfully and religiously abide by and conform to such determination as should there be entered into, and come from thence recommended."

This effort failing of success, on the 9th of February, 1775, at a meeting of the inhabitants of St. John's Parish, — convened at Midway and presided over by Lyman Hall, — Joseph Wood, Daniel Roberts, and Samuel Stevens, members of the parish committee, were deputed with a carefully prepared letter to repair to Charlestown, South Carolina, and request of the Committee of Correspondence their "permission to form an alliance with them, and to conduct trade and commerce according to the Act of Non-importation to which they had already acceded." Among other arguments advanced in that communication, framed and signed by Dr. Hall as chairman, we find the following: —

"Our being a parish of a non-associated province cannot, we presume, prevent our joining the other provinces, as the restrictions mentioned in the 14th clause of the General Association must, as we apprehend, be considered as a general rule only, and respects this province considered in a mixed or promiscuous sense; but as we of this parish are a body detached from the rest by our resolutions and association, and sufficiently distinct by local situation, large enough for particular notice, and have been treated as such by a particular address from the late Continental Congress, adjoining a seaport, and in that respect capable of conforming to the General Association, and (if connected with you) with the same fidelity as a distinct parish of your own province: therefore we must be considered as comprehended within the spirit and equitable meaning of the Continental Association, and we are assured you will not condemn the innocent with the guilty, especially when a due separation is made between them."

Reaching Charlestown on the 23d of February, Messrs. Wood, Roberts, and Stevens waited upon the General Committee and earnestly endeavored to accomplish their mission. While expressing their admiration of the patriotism of the parish, and entreating its citizens to persevere in their laudable exertions, the Carolinians deemed it "a violation of the Continental Association to remove the prohibition in favor of any *part* of a province."

Disappointed, and yet not despairing, the inhabitants of St. John's Parish "resolved to prosecute their claims to an equality with the Confederated Colonies." Having adopted certain resolutions by which they obligated themselves to hold no commerce with Savannah or other places except under the supervision of a committee, and then only with a view to procuring the necessaries of life, and having avowed their entire sympathy with all the articles and declarations promulgated by the General Congress, the inhabitants of St. John's Parish elected Dr. Lyman Hall as a delegate to represent them in the Continental Congress. This appointment occurred on the 21st of March, 1775, and was conferred in direct recognition of his prominent and persistent services in behalf of the revolutionists. No more suitable selection could have been made. Among the prominent citizens of the parish no one enjoyed a more enviable reputation for courage, ability, wisdom, and loyalty to the aims of the republican party. When departing for the Continental Congress, he carried with him, as a present from his constituents to the suffering patriots in Massachusetts, one hundred and sixty barrels of rice and fifty pounds sterling.

The patriotic spirit of its inhabitants, and this independent action of St. John's Parish in advance of the other Georgia parishes, were afterwards acknowledged when all the parishes were in accord in the revolutionary movement. As a tribute of praise, and in token of general admiration, the name of *Liberty County* was conferred upon the consolidated parishes of St. John, St. Andrew, and St. James. On the 13th of May, 1775, Dr. Hall, who had been so instrumental in persuading the Parish of St. John to this independent course, attended at the door of Congress, presented his credentials, and was unanimously "admitted *as a delegate from the Parish of St. John in the Colony of Georgia*, subject to such regulations as Congress should determine relative to his voting." Until Georgia was fully represented, he declined to vote upon questions which were to be decided by a vote of colonies. He participated, however, in the debates, recorded his opinion in cases where an expression of sentiment by colonies was not required, and declared his earnest conviction "that the example which had been shown by the parish which he represented would be speedily followed, and that the representation of Georgia would soon be complete."

This came to pass within a very few months, and Georgia assumed her station and responsibilities in the sisterhood of Confederated Colonies.

By successive appointments Dr. Hall was continued as a member from Georgia of the Continental Congress. Upon the fall of Savannah in December, 1778, and the capture of Sunbury, the entire coast region of Georgia passed into the possession of the king's forces, which overran, plundered, and exacted the most onerous tribute. To the families of those who maintained their allegiance to the rebel cause no mercy was shown. Stripped of property, their homes rendered desolate, often without food and clothing, they were dependent upon the charity of impoverished neighbors.

Dr. Hall's residence in Sunbury and his rice plantation near Midway Meeting-House were despoiled. Under such melancholy circumstances he removed his family to the North, and there resided until the evacuation of Savannah in 1782. While his services as a member of the Continental Congress were perhaps not as conspicuous as those rendered by some of his brethren, it may nevertheless be fairly claimed that he was regular, earnest, and intelligent in the discharge of the important duties devolving upon him. He was present, and in association with Button Gwinnett and George Walton affixed his signature to the Declaration of Independence.

Between Dr. Hall and the gifted, ambitious Gwinnett existed a warm friendship. The former resided at Sunbury, and the latter upon St. Catherine Island, within distant sight of that pleasant village. They constantly exchanged social courtesies, and were of one mind upon the political questions which then agitated and divided the public thought. As president of the Council of Safety and Commander-in-Chief of Georgia, Gwinnett, in 1777, anxious to signalize his administration by a feat of arms, planned an expedition for the subjugation of East Florida. Instead of intrusting the command of the forces employed to General Lachlan McIntosh, who, as the ranking military officer of Georgia, was entitled in all fairness and in accordance with custom to expect and to claim it, Gwinnett set him aside and determined in person to lead the expedition. McIntosh was not even permitted to accompany his brigade, and Colonel Elbert was assigned to the command of the Continental forces to the exclusion of his superior officer. General McIntosh was naturally incensed at this conduct of Gwinnett, and denounced him in unmeasured terms.

Soon after, when, in the exercise of his gubernatorial powers and responding to the emergency caused by the lamented death of Archibald Bulloch, Gwinnett convened the Legislature to elect his successor, McIntosh espoused the choice of John Adam Treutlen, who was the rival candidate for popular favor. Gwinnett had set his heart upon the office, and was grievously disappointed at the selection of his opponent. So violent was the animosity harbored by McIntosh, that, during the short but heated canvass, he publicly denounced Gwinnett in unmeasured terms. The quarrel between these gentlemen culminated on the 15th of May, 1777, when Gwinnett challenged McIntosh to mortal combat. They met the next morning at sunrise within the present limits of the city of Savannah. What then transpired we relate in the language of Dr. Hall, who, in a postscript to a letter addressed to the Hon. Roger Sherman, under date of Savannah, June 1, 1777, writes as follows:—

"I resume my Pen to confirm what you have no Doubt heard, that our worthy Friend Gwinnett has unfortunately fell. The Contention between him & the Genl run high, principally respectg the Expedition against E. Florida, which brot on an Enquiry in the House of Assembly into the Conduct of Mr Gwinnett who, as President & Commander in Chief, had made the preparations & meant with the Militia, and aid of Continentl Troops, to have carried them into Execution as principal Leader & Commander: he proceeded as far as Sunbury, — from this about 40 mile, — with a small Fleet, from thence sent for the Militia and Continentl Troops to join him — few of the Militia turned out, except those of the Parish of St. John, & when the Genl with the Continentl Troops arrived, Mr Gwinnett summoned a Council of War, but the Genl it seems would not hold a Council of War with him: he repeated his Summonses, but to no purpose, on which Mr. Gwinnet's Council & the Field Officers of the Genl advised both to return to this place and leave the command of the Expedition to the next Officer. This matter was laid before the Assembly, where both appeared and were heard, on which the Assembly Resolved 'that they approved the Conduct of Mr Gwinnett & his Council so far as those matters had been laid before them.' Here it was (in Assembly) that the Genl called him (as 't is said) *a Scoundrell & lying Rascal* — I confess I did not hear the words, not being so nigh the parties; however it seems agreed that it was so. A Duel was the consequence, in whh they were placed at 10 or 12 foot Distance. Discharged their Pistols nearly at the same Time. Each wounded in the Thigh. Mr Gwinnett's thigh broke so that he fell — on whh ('t is said) the Gen[l] Asked him if he chose to take another shot—was answered Yes, if they would help him up (or words nearly the same). The seconds interposed. M[r] Gwinnett was brought in, the Weather Extremely hot. A Mortification came on—he languish'd from that Morning (Friday) till Monday Morning following, & expired.

"O Liberty! Why do you suffer so many of your faithful sons, your warmest Votaries, to fall at your Shrine! Alas! my Friend, my Friend!

. . . .

"Excuse me, D[r] Sir, the Man was *Valuable*, so attached to the Liberty of this State & Continent that his whole Attention, Influence, & Interest centered in it, & seemed riveted to it. He left a Mournful Widow and Daugh[r] & I may say the Friends of Liberty on a whole Continent to deplore his Fall." . . .

Gwinnett's death caused intense excitement. Dr. Hall—one of his executors and a warm personal friend—and other gentlemen of influence brought the matter to the notice of the Legislature, and charged the judicial officers with a neglect of duty in not arresting McIntosh and binding him over to answer to the charge of murder. Informed of these facts, so soon as his wound permitted, the general surrendered himself to Judge Glen, entered into bonds for his appearance, was indicted, tried, and acquitted. Even this determination of the matter did not allay the resentment of the Gwinnett party, who, incensed at the loss of their leader, used every exertion to impair the influence of McIntosh and to fetter his efforts in the public service. At the suggestion of his friends, he repaired to the headquarters of General Washington for assignment to duty in other quarters. For nearly two years he remained absent from his native State.

Upon his return to Georgia, Dr. Hall selected Savannah as his home, and, with shattered fortunes, resumed the practice of his profession. While thus quietly employed he was, in January, 1783, elected Governor of Georgia.

His acknowledgment of the honor thus conferred was expressed in the following brief inaugural address:

"Mr. Speaker and Gentlemen of the House of Assembly:

"I esteem your unsolicited appointment of me to the office of Chief Magistrate of this State as the greatest honor, and I am affected with sentiments of the warmest gratitude on this occasion. The early and decided part which I took in the cause of America originated from a full conviction of the justice and rectitude of the cause we engaged in, has uniformly continued as the principle of my heart, and I trust will to the last moments of my life.

"If I can, by a strict attention to the various objects of government, and a steady and impartial exertion of the powers with which you have invested me, carry into execution the wise and salutary laws of the State, it will afford a pleasing prospect of our future welfare, brighten the dawn of independence, and establish the genuine principles of whigism on a firm and permanent foundation.

"The confident reliance, gentlemen, I have in the wisdom of the council you have assigned me, and the firm support of your honorable House, afford a flattering expectation of succeeding in this difficult and important trust."

Georgia had but recently emerged from the perils and privations of the Revolution; and, while all were rejoicing in the inchoate blessings of independence, poverty, sorrow, and desolation were the heritage of many homes. The energies of his administration, which lasted for only one year, were chiefly directed to the establishment of land offices and the sale of confiscated property; to the arrangement of the public debt, and the rewarding of officers and soldiers with bounty warrants for services rendered; with the accommodation of differences and the prevention of further disturbance with Florida, and the adjustment of the northern boundary of Georgia; with the establishment of courts and schools; and with the consummation of treaties of cession from and amity with contiguous Indian nations. The most important of these were solemnized at Augusta with the Cherokee Indians in May, and with the Creek Indians in November, 1783. Upon the assembling of the Legislature at Augusta, on the 8th of July, 1783, Governor Hall, in his message, thus commended to its members the subject of public education:—

"In addition, therefore, to wholesome laws restraining vice, every encouragement ought to be given to introduce religion, and learned clergy to perform divine worship in honor of God, and to cultivate principles of religion and virtue among our citizens. For this purpose it will be your wisdom to lay an early foundation for endowing seminaries of learning; nor can you, I conceive, lay a better than by a grant of a sufficient tract of land, that may, as in other governments, hereafter, by lease or otherwise, raise a revenue sufficient to support such valuable institutions."

Be it spoken and remembered to his perpetual praise

that Governor Hall, by this early and wise suggestion, sounded the key-note and paved the way for the foundation and the sustentation of the University of Georgia, which, for nearly a century, has proven the parent of higher education and civilization in Georgia. Upon the conclusion of his term of service he resumed, in Savannah, the practice of his profession, holding no public office save that of judge of the inferior court of Chatham County. This position he resigned upon his removal to Burke County in 1790. He had evidently prospered and accumulated a fortune somewhat unusual in that day and community, for he then purchased a fine plantation on the Savannah River, not far from Shell Bluff, and furnished it with a considerable number of negro slaves, and all animals, implements, and provisions requisite for its proper cultivation.

Here he died on the 19th of October, 1790, in the sixty-seventh year of his age, leaving a widow Mary, and a son John (both of whom within a short time followed him to the tomb), and was buried in a substantial brick vault situated on a bold bluff overlooking the Savannah River. There he rested until his remains were removed and brought to Augusta, Georgia, and placed, in association with those of George Walton, beneath the monument erected by patriotic citizens in front of the court house in honor of the signers from Georgia of the Declaration of Independence. Gwinnett's bones could not be found; for, although it was believed that he was interred in the old cemetery on South Broad Street in Savannah, no stone having been erected over his grave, all memory of the place of his sepulture had vanished.

The will of Dr. Hall, which was on file in the office of the Court of Ordinary of Burke County, at Waynesboro', was destroyed by an accidental fire which consumed the court house and most of the public records. Subsequent to the removal of his remains to Augusta, Mr. William D'Antignac, who then owned the Hall plantation, forwarded to the corporate authorities of Wallingford, Connecticut, the native town of the signer, the marble slab inserted in the front of the brick vault wherein they had so long rested. That slab is still carefully preserved. It bears the following inscription:—

Beneath this stone rest the remains of

HON. LYMAN HALL,

formerly Governor of this State, who departed this life on the 19th of October, 1790, in the 67th year of his age. In the cause of America he was uniformly a patriot. In the incumbent duties of a husband and a father he acquitted himself with affection and tenderness.

But reader, above all know from this inscription that he left this probationary state as a true Christian and an honest man.

To those so mourned in death, so loved in life,
The childless parent and the widowed wife
With tears inscribes this monumental stone,
That holds his ashes and expects her own.

In Sanderson's "Lives of the Signers" we are advised that Dr. Lyman Hall was six feet high and finely proportioned; that his manners were easy and polite; that his deportment was affable and dignified; that the force of his enthusiasm was tempered by discretion; that he was firm in purpose and principles; that the ascendency which he gained was engendered by a mild, persuasive manner coupled with a calm, unruffled temper;

and that, possessing a strong, discriminating mind, he had the power of imparting his energy to others, and was peculiarly fitted to flourish in the perplexing and perilous scenes of the Revolution.

While there are several engraved portraits of this signer, we cannot speak authoritatively in regard to the genuineness of any of them. Careful inquiry has thus far failed to disclose the existence of any original portrait of Dr. Hall, unless that in the Philadelphia group, from which my friend Dr. Thomas Addis Emmet, of New York city, had his drawing made, may be so regarded. So far as we can ascertain, there is in Georgia no original likeness of Dr. Hall. His only son died childless, and there are no lineal descendants of this signer. The State of Georgia perpetuates his name by one of her counties, and the memory of his manly walk and conversation, of his Christian virtues, useful acts, and patriotic impulses, is and will be gratefully cherished.

Although he never bore arms, or won the distinction of an orator, he hazarded everything in the cause of humanity and liberty, on every occasion manifesting an exalted patriotism conscious of the blessings to be secured and jealous of the rights to be defended.

JOHN HOUSTOUN.

THIS son of Sir Patrick Houstoun, Bart., — registrar of grants, receiver of quitrents, and a member of council under the royal government in Georgia, — was a lawyer by profession and a gentleman of liberal education, culture, and refinement. He was born in the Parish of St. George on the 31st of August, 1744. Repudiating that allegiance to the Crown which his father and many of the older and prominent citizens of the Colony so earnestly cherished and steadfastly maintained, at an early period he avowed sentiments of disloyalty to the acts of Parliament, and espoused the cause of the rebels. In July, 1774, we find him, with Noble W. Jones, Archibald Bulloch, and John Walton, extending a public invitation to all the inhabitants of Georgia to meet at the Liberty Pole, at Tondee's Tavern, in Savannah, to consider their constitutional rights and liberties as American subjects, and to adopt such measures for the redress of existing grievances as might appear proper and expedient. By those who responded to the call Mr. Houstoun was appointed a member of a committee to prepare resolutions, similar to those which had been passed by the Northern Colonies, expressive of their condemnation of the recent unjust and oppressive acts of Parliament, and of their determination to employ all lawful means for the assertion of their constitutional rights. The 10th of the following August was fixed as the day, and the town of Savannah was designated as the place, for the submission, by the committee, of the desired report.

In contempt of the wish of Governor Wright, and in utter disregard of his proclamation denouncing the purposed assemblage as illegal and revolutionary, a general meeting of the inhabitants of the Province was held at Tondee's Tavern at the time suggested. The committee then reported a series of resolutions, very independent in their tone, and expressive of sentiments favorable to the redress of pending political ills and to a union of the Province with her twelve sisters in a confederation for the common defense. Of the committee then raised to solicit and forward supplies for the relief of the impoverished Bostonians, Mr. Houstoun was a member.

The conclusions reached and promulgated by this convocation of liberty-loving people provoked severe comment on the part of the king's servants, intensified the division of sentiment upon the political questions which then agitated the popular mind, and evoked violent protests from various quarters. In that meeting the propriety of sending six deputies to the General Congress of the American Colonies had been discussed, but the suggestion did not meet with general favor.

Resolved upon controlling the political fortunes of the Province, and intent upon moulding public sentiment to their will, the "Sons of Liberty" called a Provincial Congress to meet on the 18th of January, 1775, at Savannah. The power of Governor Wright, and of the loyal party in Georgia, had been so successfully exerted in preventing a general response to the invitation extended by the patriots of Christ Church Parish, that, upon the assembling of that Provincial Congress, only five of the twelve parishes composing the Colony were represented by delegates, and some of them were so hampered by restrictions that their freedom of expression and action was materially impaired. Chagrined at the inaction of the Province, the delegates present essayed to accomplish through the Commons House of Assembly, then in session, that which, of themselves, they were not strong enough to perform. In this, however, they were defeated by the action of Governor Wright, who, by adjourning the Assembly, thwarted the design of the Liberty party, and prevented a nomination of delegates to the Continental Congress, which, had it been made by the Assembly, would have carried with it at least the apparent sanction of the entire Province. Nevertheless, the Provincial Congress, feeble as it was, did nominate Mr. Houstoun, Archibald Bulloch, and Dr. Noble W. Jones to represent Georgia in the Continental Congress. Rightly judging, however, that an election by a minority of the parishes did not justify a claim on their part to represent the entire Province, those gentlemen did not attempt to take their seats in the Continental Congress to which they had been thus accredited, but contented themselves with addressing a carefully prepared communication to the president of that body, in which they suggested reasons in explanation of the course adopted by them.

On the 21st of June, by a call over their own signatures, Dr. Noble W. Jones, Archibald Bulloch, John Houstoun, and George Walton, requested the inhabitants of the town and district of Savannah to meet at the Liberty Pole, at ten o'clock in the forenoon of the following day, to select a committee to bring about a union of Georgia with the other American Colonies. At the appointed place and designated hour many were present; a Council of Safety was then chosen, with instructions to maintain an active correspondence with the Continental Congress, with Councils of Safety in other Provinces, and with committees in other Georgia parishes, with a view to the consummation of the proposed union. Similar meetings were held in Georgia, all looking to an early affiliation with the confederated sisterhood of American Colonies. As a result of these combined efforts on the part of the patriots, there assembled in Savannah on the 4th of July, 1775, a Provincial Congress in which every Georgia parish was fully and ably represented. In the deliberations of this Congress, Mr. Houstoun — who was present as a delegate from the town and district of Savannah — actively participated. By the conclusions then reached, Georgia was at length placed in full communion and alliance with the twelve other American Colonies. Of the delegates then selected to represent this Province in the Continental Congress, Mr. Houstoun was the first chosen. Responding to this important trust, he journeyed to Philadelphia, and there, with Messrs. Bulloch and Zubly, participated in the deliberations of that body at a session convened in September.

Mr. Houstoun was similarly complimented by the Provincial Congress which assembled in Savannah in January, 1776, and again by the Congress which convened in the fall of that year. Of the Executive Council, of which Benjamin Andrew was chosen president, he was a member, when, on the 10th of January, 1778, he was elected Governor of Georgia. But for the defection of Dr. Zubly, which necessitated Mr. Houstoun's presence in Georgia at that perilous epoch, his name would have been affixed to the Declaration of Independence.

While Charlestown was still rejoicing over the defeat of the British fleet before the palmetto-covered walls of the fort on Sullivan's Island, in company with Jonathan Bryan and Colonel Lachlan McIntosh, Mr. Houstoun waited upon General Charles Lee, and, in the name of the Council of Safety of Georgia, besought his assistance in repelling the constantly occurring incursions from Florida. After recounting the numerous depredations committed on the southern and southwestern frontiers of Georgia by lawless bands swarming from Florida, and the desolation wrought along the coast by privateers commissioned by Governor Tonyn, the committee suggested a plan of operations by which these banditti might be slain or dispersed, and the town of St. Augustine captured. Moved by the representations of the committee, General Lee resolved upon an expedition for the relief of Georgia, which, although subsequently inaugurated, was not prosecuted to a successful conclusion.

When Mr. Houstoun was inducted into office as Governor of Georgia, the southern frontier of the State was intensely excited, and serious apprehensions were entertained that the entire commonwealth would be overrun and plundered by British, Tories, and Indians issuing from East Florida. At a meeting of the Executive Council held on the 16th of April to consider the attitude of affairs, both civil and military, an extraordinary political act was committed. It was nothing less than investing the governor with almost dictatorial powers. In a preamble and resolutions, that council declared the situation in Georgia to be so truly alarming that only the most spirited and vigorous exertions could suffice to defeat the machinations of the enemy; and that "in such times of danger it might happen that everything would depend upon instantaneous measures being embraced, which could not be done should the governor wait for calling a council." Having then recorded their favorable opinion of the constitutionality of the measure they proposed to adopt, the members proceeded to sanction the following unusual and dangerous policy: "The Council, therefore, impressed with a sense of the calamitous situation of this State, and apprehending it as an unavoidable expedient, do request that his Honor the Governor will be pleased to take upon himself to act in such manner as to him shall seem most eligible; and to exercise all the executive powers of government appertaining to the militia, or the defense of the State against the present danger which threatens it, or in annoyance of the enemy, independent of the Executive Council, and without calling, consulting, or advising with them, unless when and where he shall find it convenient and shall choose to do so. And they pledge themselves to support and uphold him in so doing, and to adopt as their own the measures which he shall embrace; and that this shall continue during the present emergency, or until the honorable House of Assembly shall make an order or give their opinion to the contrary."

To this remarkable exhibition of personal confidence

Governor Houstoun replied: "He was exceedingly unwilling to do any act without the approbation of the Council; but that as he found, by experience during the present alarm, the impossibility of at all times getting them together when too much, perhaps, depended upon a minute, and further that as the Council had given it as their opinion that the proceeding was justifiable under the Constitution, and as the meeting of the Assembly was so near at hand and alarms and dangers seemed to thicken on all sides, he agreed to act in the manner the Council requested, during the present emergency, or until the honorable House of Assembly should make an order or give their opinion to the contrary."

While such a delegation of authority may not have been prohibited in terms by the Constitution of 1777, it is very questionable whether the framers of that instrument ever contemplated such a cession on the part of the members of the Executive Council who were constituted the special advisers and coadjutors of the governor in the exercise of the executive powers of government.

The threatening aspect of affairs on the Southern frontier, and the general alarm pervading the State, caused this abnormal action on the part of the Executive Council.

East Florida, with its king's forces, Scovilites, outlaws, and subsidized Indians, was a thorn in the side of Georgia. St. Augustine, as the military hive whence these predatory bands swarmed to the annoyance of the dwellers between the Alatamaha and the St. Mary rivers, was an object of constant disquietude and hatred. Its destruction was a favorite scheme with the

Georgia authorities. What General Lee and Governor Gwinnett had failed to accomplish, Governor Houstoun was ambitious to achieve. Invested by the Executive Council with powers little less than dictatorial, he desired to inaugurate and conduct an expedition which would render his administration famous, and minister to the security of the commonwealth over which he presided. Strengthened by a recent accession of Tories from the heart of South Carolina, the Floridians were preparing for another and a formidable incursion into Georgia. Of this fact Governor Houstoun was informed, and his desire was not only to push back this hostile column, but to follow up his advantage even to the investment and occupation of St. Augustine.

Upon a conference with General Robert Howe, who was then in command of the Southern Department, with his headquarters at Savannah, it was resolved to concentrate the military strength of Georgia for repelling the threatened attack, and for the subsequent invasion of Florida. Of the militia of the State, Governor Houstoun proposed to take and retain personal command. When summoned to the field, they did not aggregate more than three hundred and fifty men, many of whom were poorly armed and badly disciplined. The Continental forces within the limits of the State numbered only about five hundred and fifty. These were supplemented by two hundred and fifty Continental infantry, and thirty artillerists with two field-pieces, drawn from South Carolina, and commanded by Colonel Charles Cotesworth Pinckney. The Carolina militia, under Colonels Bull and Williamson, were ordered to rendezvous at Purrysburg, on the

Savannah River. Fort Howe, on the Alatamaha, was designated as the place for concentration.

Upon the details of this expedition, including the gallant capture of the Hinchinbrooke and the Rebecca by Colonel Elbert; the brave but fruitless attempt of Colonel Clarke to dislodge the enemy from his fortified position on Alligator Creek; the tardy movements of the militia; the suffering engendered by a malarial region, intense heat, bad water, insufficient shelter, deficient transportation, and unwholesome food; the distractions consequent upon disagreements between commanding officers, and the deplorable effects of a lack of military discipline, we may not dwell. Remembering the powers conferred by his Executive Council, Governor Houstoun, with his militia, refused to receive orders from General Howe. Colonel Williamson's troops would not yield obedience to a Continental officer, and Commodore Bowen insisted that the naval forces were entirely distinct from, and independent of, the land service. Thus was General Howe left to rely only upon the Continental troops. Had a masterly mind been present, quickly would these discordant elements have been consolidated; rapidly, by stern orders and enforced discipline, would the army in all its parts have been unified and brought into efficient subjection. But there was no potent voice to evoke order out of confusion,—no iron will to dominate over the emergency. Discouraged by the perplexing delays, appalled by the sickness of the troops, embarrassed by the want of coöperation among the commanders, the lack of stores, and the inefficiency of the transportation department, and uncertain as to the future, General Howe convened a council of war at

Fort Tonyn, on the 11th of July, which advised an abandonment of the expedition so far as the Continental forces were concerned.

Left to themselves by the withdrawal of the Continental troops, Governor Houstoun and Colonel Williamson, with the Georgia and South Carolina militia, at first contemplated an advance as far as the river St. John. This purpose, however, conceived in a spirit of pride and vainglory, was speedily abandoned, and the men under their command were led back by land and dispersed to their respective homes.

The most that can be said in favor of this campaign, with its lamentable lack of preparation, want of management, disagreement between commanders, surprising mistakes, inexcusable delays, vexatious disappointments, and fruitless expenditures of men and munitions, is that it prevented for a season the advance of the enemy from Florida. Whether this sufficiently atoned for the waste of time, health, life, and treasure may fairly be questioned.

In 1784 Mr. Houstoun was a second time elected Governor of Georgia. It was during this administration that provision was made by the legislature for the establishment of a State institution of learning, which — at first as Franklin College, and subsequently as the University of Georgia — has, for nearly a century, moulded the higher education of the youths of this commonwealth, and ministered to the civilization of Georgia. The original cession of forty thousand acres of the public lands for the foundation and support of this school was made to Governor Houstoun, James Habersham, William Few, Joseph Clay, Abraham Baldwin, William Houstoun, and Nathan Brownson, in trust for the purpose designated; and Governor Houstoun was first named in the list of trustees who, in 1785, were empowered to put this educational scheme in practical operation.

Much attention was now bestowed upon issuing warrants to such citizens as had rendered military service during the late war, and in the orderly administration of the Land Court.

In 1786 Mr. Houstoun was commissioned as Chief Justice of Georgia, and in the following year he was a member of the commission appointed by the State to settle the boundary line between Georgia and South Carolina. In the convention, which concluded its labors at Beaufort, South Carolina, on the 28th of April, 1787, Georgia was represented by Governor Houstoun, Major John Habersham, and General Lachlan McIntosh; while, on the part of South Carolina, General Charles Cotesworth Pinckney, General Andrew Pickens, and the Hon. Pierce Butler appeared as commissioners. From the conclusions arrived at by that commission Governor Houstoun dissented, and his reasons for such dissent may be found *in extenso* in Marbury and Crawford's Digest, pp. 666 and 677. Like everything which emanated from his pen, this document is clear, forcible, and well expressed.

In 1789 he was voted for under the operation of the Constitution just promulgated, but the choice for Governor was accorded to the Hon. Edward Telfair. The same year Mr. Houstoun was elected a justice for Chatham County, and in the following year he was complimented with the Mayoralty of Savannah. Upon the occasion of President Washington's visit to that city, in May, 1791, he was a member of the committee which welcomed and entertained the illustrious guest.

While not busied with public affairs Governor Houstoun clave to his profession, of which he was an ornament, and in the practice of which he always found lucrative and honorable employment. No citizen enjoyed a more enviable reputation, or commended himself more thoroughly to the confidence and the respect of the community. Many important trusts were committed to his keeping. In their execution he was uniformly faithful and competent. He died at his suburban home at White Bluff, near Savannah, on the 20th of July, 1796.[1] Georgia perpetuates his name and his memory by one of her largest and most fertile counties.

[1] Two days afterwards his will was admitted to probate. It remains of file and of record in the Ordinary's Office of Chatham County, in Savannah, Georgia.

WILLIAM HOUSTOUN.

THE subject of this sketch — a son of Sir Patrick Houstoun, and a brother of Governor John Houstoun — is believed to have been born in Savannah, where his life was spent. He was a lawyer by profession, having been admitted in 1776 to the Inner Temple, London. Returning home, he espoused the cause of ·the Revolutionists, and was twice honored by selection as a Delegate to the Continental Congress. In 1787 he was chosen as one of the deputies from Georgia to the convention for revising the Federal Constitution. Although he attended and participated in the deliberations of that august body, his name does not appear among the members who signed the Constitution then formulated. Two years before, he had acted as one of the agents named on the part of the State of Georgia to settle the boundary between that commonwealth and Carolina. With the final adjudication of the question, however, he had no connection. His name appears among the original trustees for the establishment of the University of Georgia; and to Lyman Hall, Governor John Houstoun, William Few, Joseph Clay, Abraham Baldwin, William Houstoun, and Nathan Brownson was the primal cession of forty thousand acres of land made by the State of Georgia for the establishment and endowment of that seminary of learning.

But little can be gleaned in regard to this member from Georgia of the Continental Congress, but the tradition lives that he was a thorough gentleman, an accomplished lawyer, and a citizen of high repute.

We are informed that his portrait, as well as that of Governor Houstoun, with the family plate and many papers of historical value, were unfortunately and accidentally consumed by fire in Southwestern Georgia, whither, during the late war between the States, they had been conveyed in the hope of promoting their safety.

RICHARD HOWLEY.

WHEN first introduced to our acquaintance, this member of the Continental Congress was a resident of St. John's Parish, where he practiced law, supplementing his professional labors by attention to a small rice plantation. Upon the fall of Sunbury, in January, 1779, and the occupation of Southern Georgia by the King's forces, he removed to St. Paul's Parish, where, in affiliation with George Wells and others opposed to the existing Executive Council, he called a convention, which, at Augusta, resolved itself into a legislative body, claimed to be the General Assembly of Georgia, chose William Glascock Speaker, and proceeded to elect George Walton Governor of the young and distracted commonwealth.

On the 4th of January, 1780, Mr. Howley was elected Governor of Georgia. Composed largely of the friends of Walton and himself, the Assembly which conferred this honor severely criticised the former Council, and accused its members of "exercising powers and authorities unknown to and subversive of the Constitution and laws of this State." It even went so far as to declare that "said Council and the powers they exercised were illegal and unconstitutional." Nevertheless, within a month this Assembly, which had thus pronounced null and void the action of the former Council, and denounced it as lawless in conception and operation, moved by the exigency of the period, and anticipating it might happen during the progress of the war "that the Ministers of Government of this State might not be able to do or transact the business of the State within the limits of the same," unanimously resolved "that his Honor the Governor, or, in his absence, the President and Executive Council, might do and transact all and every business of government in as full, ample, and authoritative manner in any other State within the Confederation, touching and respecting of this State, as though it had been done and transacted within the limits of this State." Fortunately, in the judgment of Governor Howley, the occasion did not arise for the exercise of this extraordinary and manifestly unauthorized power.

Informed of the arrival of reinforcements to the British troops in Savannah, — the ultimate destination of which was not then well ascertained, — the Governor issued a stirring proclamation, "commanding and requiring the people to stand firm to their duty, and exert themselves in support and defense of the great and glorious independency of the United States; and also to remember with gratitude to Heaven that the Almighty Ruler of human affairs hath been pleased to raise up the spirit and might of the two greatest powers in the world [France and Spain] to join with them and oppose and destroy the persecutor of their liberties and immunities."

General Lincoln was censured for withdrawing the Continental troops from Georgia, and was pronounced "answerable for all the consequences which might follow that unadvised measure." Governor Howley was instructed to concentrate half the militia of the State at Augusta, and Colonel John Twiggs, with his command and as many volunteers as he could secure, was ordered to take post at that point.

Aware of the defenseless condition of this town, "which might be surprised by twenty men," and deeming it "unsafe and impolitic for the Governor and Council to remain thus exposed," the Assembly designated Heard's Fort, in Wilkes County, as a suitable "place of meeting for transacting the business of the government of this State as soon after leaving Augusta as may be."

Responding to this suggestion, the Governor and Executive Council did, on the 5th of February, adjourn to Heard's Fort, which thereupon became the temporary capital of the State. Brief was the gubernatorial term of Governor Howley. He soon left Georgia to take his seat in the Continental Congress; and the Hon. George Wells — the President of Council — and three members of the Board were announced as competent for the transaction of all public business. Republican Georgia at this time could practically claim the full allegiance of only two counties, — Richmond and Wilkes, — and its condition was indeed deplorable. Driven from Savannah and the seaboard, compelled to evacuate Augusta, hemmed in by hostile Indians on the frontier, confronted by British Regulars and Tories, harassed with alarms, surprised by ambuscades, and pinched with want, the patriots were engaged in a long and bitter struggle for simple existence, with scarcely a ray of hope to light up the future.

So depreciated was the paper money of the State that Governor Howley, in making his way to Congress, in the language of Captain McCall, dealt it out by the quire for a night's lodging for himself and party; "and if the fare was anything extraordinary, the landlord was compensated with two quires."

At this darkest epoch, when English arms had gained the ascendency not only in Georgia but also in South Carolina, when the principal towns of those States were in the possession of the enemy and the territory on both sides of the Savannah River was largely subservient to British rule, it was noised abroad that a new commission would soon issue from the Court of St. James for the purpose of again sounding the temper of America upon the subject of a pacification. It was boldly hinted that in any negotiations Georgia, and perhaps South Carolina, would not be recognized as parts of the American Union, but that they would be excluded, on the ground that they "had been again colonized to England by new conquest." In Europe the *uti possidetis* was much talked of as "a probable basis for the anticipated peace." Against this doctrine and its practical application George Walton, William Few, and Richard Howley — then representing Georgia in the Continental Congress — prepared and published a manly and earnest protest,[1] which was not without its influence.

Upon the conclusion of peace Governor Howley returned to his home in Liberty County, where he resumed the practice of his profession. Prior to his death, which occurred in Savannah, Georgia, in December, 1784, he had become a resident of that town. His will — now of file in the Ordinary's Office of Chatham County — bears date on the 6th of that month, and was probated on the 4th of January, 1785.

[1] *Observations upon the Effects of Certain Late Political Suggestions by the Delegates of Georgia*, pp. 10. Philadelphia, MDCCLXXXI.

NOBLE WYMBERLEY JONES.

THIS son of Colonel Noble Jones, a trusted friend and early companion of Oglethorpe, — who, as military officer, surveyor, registrar, member of the Royal Council, and treasurer of the Province of Georgia, during a long life proved himself a valuable and an influential citizen, and never once wavered in his allegiance to the Crown, — was born near London, England, in 1723.

Such was the respect and so great was the affection entertained for him by his distinguished and devoted son that, when first elected a member from Georgia of the Continental Congress, Noble W. Jones, in deference to the entreaties of his aged father, then sorely perplexed and trembling upon the verge of the grave, put aside for the time being this important trust, that he might, with filial love, minister to the infirmities and soothe the last hours of his dying parent.

Coming to Georgia at a tender age, he secured a cadet's appointment in Oglethorpe's regiment. Having in time studied medicine and received his degree, he was promoted to a first lieutenancy, and, with the rank and pay of surgeon, was assigned to a company of Rangers in the pay of the Crown. After a few years passed in military service, he resigned from the army, and entered upon the practice of his profession in Savannah. He rose rapidly in the public esteem, as a citizen and as a physician winning golden opinions from the community. No idle spectator of passing events, or indifferent to political preferment, he was in 1768 elected Speaker of the Lower House of Assembly of the Province of Georgia. By that body he was placed upon a committee to correspond with Dr. Benjamin Franklin — who had been appointed an agent "to represent, solicit, and transact the affairs of the Colony of Georgia in Great Britain" — and give such instructions as might appear necessary for the public welfare. Reëlected to this position in 1770, so pronounced and influential had become his views and conduct in opposition to the objectionable and oppressive acts of Parliament and in support of American ideas that Governor Wright, exercising the power vested in him, refused to sanction this choice, and ordered the House to select another Speaker.

Incensed at this affront offered to one who has been aptly termed a morning star of liberty in Georgia, and resenting what they deemed an unwarrantable interference with the power resting solely with them to nominate and judge of the qualification of their own presiding officer, the members of the House passed resolutions complimentary to Dr. Jones, and declared "that the sense and approbation this House entertain of his conduct can never be lessened by any slight cast upon him in opposition to the unanimous voice of the Commons House of Assembly in particular and the Province in general." Criticising the action of the Executive, they resolved "that this rejection by the Governor of a Speaker unanimously elected was a high breach of the privileges of the House, and tended to subvert the most valuable rights and liberties of the people and their representatives." This bold assertion the Council was pleased to stigmatize as "a most indecent and insolent denial of his Majesty's authority," and the Governor, wielding the only punitive weapon at command, dissolved the Assembly on the 22d of February, 1770.

Adhering to the preference shown on a former occasion, and resolved to rebuke the late interference on the part of the Executive, at the first session of the eighth General Assembly of the Province, convened at Savannah on the 21st of April, 1772, the Commons House perfected its organization by electing Dr. Jones as its Speaker. Officially informed of this action, the Hon. James Habersham, who during the absence of Sir James Wright was occupying the gubernatorial chair, responded: "I have his Majesty's commands to put a negative upon the Speaker now elected by the Commons House, which I accordingly do; and desire that you will inform the House that I direct them to proceed to a new choice of Speaker."

Despite this inhibition, and in direct opposition to the injunction of the Executive, thrice did the House adhere to its selection; and it was only by dissolving the Assembly that the Governor was able to carry his point.

In a long letter to the Earl of Hillsborough, dated the 30th of April, 1772, Governor Habersham dwells upon the injurious effects of this dissolution of the Assembly, and yet demonstrates its necessity in obedience to existing instructions from the Crown. He also comments freely upon the conduct of Dr. Jones and his friends in "opposing the public business" under the "specious pretence of Liberty and Privilege." "My Lord," he continues, "it is very painful to me to say or even to insinuate a disrespectful word of any one; and every person who knows me will acknowledge that it is contrary to my disposition to dip my pen in gall, but I cannot help considering Mr. Jones's conduct for some time past in opposing Public Business as very ungrateful and unworthy a good man, as his family have reaped more advantages from Government than any I know in this Province. He was several years First Lieutenant and Surgeon of a company of Rangers paid by the Crown, and in these capacities met with great indulgence. His father is the King's Treasurer, and, if I am not mistaken, reaps very considerable emoluments from it."

The truth is, while Governor Habersham was loyally seeking to carry out the instructions of the King and to support the authority of Parliament, Dr. Jones was in active sympathy with those who esteemed taxation without representation as wholly unauthorized, and who were very jealous in the maintenance of what they regarded as the reserved rights of the colonists and the privileges of provincial legislatures. Both were true men, but they viewed the situation from different standpoints. An honored servant of the Crown, Mr. Habersham was confronted with peculiar duties and stringent oaths. Dr. Jones, on the contrary, as a representative elected by the people, was free to give expression to his own and the sentiments of his constituents at an epoch when American liberty was being freely discussed and proclaimed. Of each it may be fairly said he was pure in purpose, wise in counsel, and fearless in action; enjoying in a conspicuous degree the esteem and the affection of the community. But their political paths henceforward diverged. The one clave to the Crown and shared its fortunes, while the other cast his lot with the Revolutionists, and became a favorite leader of the patriot band.

With Archibald Bulloch, John Houstoun, and John Walton, he issued the public call on the 20th of July, 1774, which convened the citizens of Georgia at the Watch House in Savannah. The resolutions then adopted and the measures there inaugurated, gathering potency and allegiance as they were discussed and comprehended, proved effective in unifying public sentiment in support of the plans suggested by the Liberty party, and paved the way for sundering the ties which bound the Province to the British Empire. Of the committees then raised to conduct the public affairs of the Colony, and to minister to the relief of the "suffering poor" of Boston, he was an active member.

Noble Wymberley Jones, Archibald Bulloch, and John Houstoun, elected delegates to the Continental Congress by a convention of patriots assembled in Savannah on the 8th of December, 1774, and again by the Provincial Congress of January, 1775, — concluding very properly that, inasmuch as they had been nominated by a political convocation which in reality embraced only four of the twelve parishes then constituting the Province of Georgia, they could not justly be regarded as representatives of the entire Colony, and yet persuaded that the will of those who commissioned them should be formally made known and the mind of Georgia be fairly interpreted, — on the 6th of April, 1775, addressed the following communication to the President of the Continental Congress: —

"Sir, — The unworthy part which the Province of Georgia has acted in the great and general contest leaves room to expect little less than the censure or even indignation of every virtuous man in America. Although, on the one hand, we feel the justice of such a consequence with respect to the Province in general, yet, on the other, we claim an exemption from it in favour of some individuals who wished a better conduct. Permit us, therefore, in behalf of ourselves and many others, our fellow citizens, warmly attached to the cause, to lay before the respectable body over which you preside a few facts which, we trust, will not only acquit us of supineness, but also render our conduct to be approved by all candid and dispassionate men.

"At the time the late Congress did this Province the honour to transmit to it an extract from their proceedings, enclosed in a friendly letter from the Honourable Mr. Middleton, the sense and disposition of the people in general seemed to fluctuate between liberty and convenience. In order to bring on a determination respecting the measures recommended, a few well-affected persons in Savannah, by public advertisement in the *Gazette*, requested a meeting of all the parishes and districts, by delegates or representatives, in Provincial Congress. On the day appointed for this meeting, with concern they found that only five out of twelve parishes to which they had particularly wrote had nominated and sent down delegates; and even some of these five had laid their representatives under injunctions as to the form of an association. Under these circumstances those who met saw themselves a good deal embarrassed. However, one expedient seemed still to present itself. The House of Assembly was then sitting, and it was hoped there would be no doubt of a majority in favour of American freedom.

The plan, therefore, was to go through with what business they could in Provincial Congress, and then, with a short address, present the same to the House of Assembly, who, it was hoped, would by votes in a few minutes and before prerogative should interfere, make it the act of the whole Province. Accordingly, the Congress framed and agreed to such an association, and did such other business as appeared practicable with the people, and had the whole just ready to be presented, when the Governor, either treacherously informed or shrewdly suspecting the step, put an end to the session. What then could the Congress do? On the one hand, truth forbid them to call their proceedings the voice of the Province, there being but five[1] out of twelve parishes concerned; and on the other, they wanted strength sufficient to enforce them on the principle of necessity, to which all ought for a time to submit. They found the inhabitants of Savannah not likely soon to give matters a favourable turn. The importers were mostly against any interruption, and the consumers very much divided. There were some of the latter virtuously for the measures; others strenuously against them; but more who called themselves neutrals than either. Thus situated, there appeared nothing before us but the alternative of either immediately commencing a civil war among ourselves, or else of patiently waiting for the measures to be recommended by the General Congress.

"Among a powerful people, provided with men, money, and conveniences, and by whose conduct others were to be regulated, the former would certainly be the resolution that would suggest itself to

[1] And one of these, St. Paul, practically withdrew.

every man removed from the condition of a coward; but in a small community like that of Savannah (whose members are mostly in their first advance towards wealth and independence, destitute of even the necessaries of life within themselves, and from whose junction or silence so little would be added or lost to the general cause), the latter presented itself as the most eligible plan, and was adopted by the people. Party disputes and animosities have occasionally prevailed, and show that the spirit of freedom is not extinguished, but only restrained for a time till an opportunity shall offer for calling it forth.

"The Congress convened at Savannah did us the honour of choosing us delegates to meet your respectable body at Philadelphia on the tenth of next month. We were sensible of the honour and weight of the appointment, and would gladly have rendered our country any service our poor abilities would have admitted of; but, alas! with what face could we have appeared for a Province whose inhabitants had refused to sacrifice the most trifling advantages to the public cause, and in whose behalf we did not think we could safely pledge ourselves for the execution of any one measure whatsoever?

"We do not mean to insinuate that those who appointed us would prove apostates or desert their opinions, but that the tide of opposition was great; that all the strength and virtue of these our friends might be sufficient for the purpose. We very early saw the difficulties that would here occur, and therefore repeatedly and constantly requested the people to proceed to the choice of other delegates in our stead; but this they refused to do. We beg, sir, you will view our reasons for not attending in a liberal point of light. Be pleased to make the most favourable representation of them to the Honourable the Members of the Congress. We believe we may take upon ourselves to say, notwithstanding all that has passed, there are still men in Georgia who, when an occasion shall require, will be ready to evince a steady, religious, and manly attachment to the liberties of America. For the consolation of these, they find themselves in the neighborhood of a Province whose virtue and magnanimity must and will do lasting honour to the cause, and in whose fate they seem disposed freely to involve their own.

"We have the honour to be, sir, your most obedient and very humble servants,

"NOBLE WYMBERLEY JONES.
"ARCHIBALD BULLOCH.
"JOHN HOUSTOUN."

The news of the affairs at Lexington and Concord reached Savannah on the 10th of May, and caused the wildest excitement. The thunders of the 19th of April aroused the Georgia parishes from their lethargy, and multiplied patriots within their borders.

The magazine at the eastern extremity of Savannah — built of brick and sunk some twelve feet under ground — contained a considerable amount of ammunition. So substantial was this structure, that Governor Wright deemed it unnecessary to post a guard for its protection. The excited Revolutionists all over the land cried aloud for powder. Impressed with the importance of securing the contents of this magazine, quietly assembling at the residence of Dr. Jones, and there hastily arranging a plan of operations, Dr. Noble W. Jones, Joseph Habersham, Edward Telfair, William Gibbons, Joseph Clay, John Milledge, and some other gentlemen, — most of them members of the Council of Safety, and all zealous in the cause of American liberty, — at a late hour on the night of the 11th of May, 1775, broke open the magazine and removed therefrom some six hundred pounds of powder, — a portion of which was sent to Beaufort, South Carolina, for safe-keeping, and the rest was concealed in the garrets and cellars of the houses of the captors. Although Governor Wright issued a proclamation offering a reward of £150 sterling for the apprehension of the offenders, it failed to elicit any information, although the actors in the affair are said to have been well known in the community. The popular heart was too deeply stirred, and the "Sons of Liberty" were too potent to tolerate any hindrance or annoyance at the hands of Royalist informers. The tradition lives, and is generally credited, that some of the powder thus obtained was forwarded to Cambridge, and was actually expended by the patriots in the memorable battle of Bunker Hill.

On the 22d of June, 1775, in response to a call signed by Dr. Jones, Archibald Bulloch, John Houstoun, and George Walton, many of the inhabitants of the town and district of Savannah assembled at the Liberty Pole in Savannah, and elected a Council of Safety, with instructions to maintain an active correspondence with the Continental Congress, and with Councils of Safety both in Georgia and in other Provinces, with a view to bringing about a union of Georgia with her sister Colonies in the cause of freedom.

Of the Provincial Congress which assembled in Savannah on the 4th of July, 1775, Dr. Jones was a member, accredited from the "Town and District of Savannah."

In this Congress every parish was represented. Dr. Jones was of the committee then selected to frame a suitable address to the inhabitants of Georgia, advising them of the true nature of the disputes existing between Great Britain and her American Colonies, and informing them of the deliberations and conclusions of the present Congress. He was also chosen, with John Houstoun, Archibald Bulloch, Reverend Dr. Zubly, and Dr. Lyman Hall, to represent Georgia in the Continental Congress. Georgia was now in acknowledged sympathy with her sisters, and took her place, by regular representation, in the National Assembly. Of the Council of Safety which ordered the arrest of Governor Wright, Dr. Jones was a member.

Late in 1776 the General Assembly of South Carolina adopted a resolution to the effect that a union between that State and Georgia would promote the general strength, wealth, and dignity, and insure mutual liberty, independence, and safety. Commissioners — of whom the Honorable William Henry Drayton appears to have been the chairman, as he certainly was the spokesman — were sent to Savannah to treat of the matter, and to secure Georgia's acquiescence in a project which, if carried into effect, would practically have put an end to her political existence. The members of the Council of Safety listened with patience and courtesy to the arguments and persuasions of the Carolina Commissioners, but rejected the proffered union. President Gwinnett, Dr. Jones, and all the leading republican spirits were radically opposed to the scheme on grounds both material and constitutional; and so the effort of South Carolina to swallow up Georgia signally miscarried.

Upon the capture of Savannah in December, 1778, Dr. Jones removed to Charles-Town, South Carolina. There, upon the fall of that city in 1780, he was taken prisoner by the British and sent in captivity to St. Augustine, Florida. Exchanged in July, 1781, he went to Philadelphia, and there entered upon the practice of his profession. While a resident of that city, he was, by the General Assembly of Georgia, reëlected to the Continental Congress.

Shortly after its evacuation by the King's forces in the summer of 1782, Dr. Jones returned to Savannah, repaired the desolations which war had wrought in his comfortable home, and resumed his professional labors. He was a member of the committee which received and saluted President Washington with an address of welcome upon the occasion of his visit to Savannah in 1791. Over the Constitutional Convention which, at Louisville, Jefferson County, in May, 1795, amended the Constitution of Georgia, Dr. Noble Wymberley Jones presided. In 1804 he was President of the Georgia Medical Society. Preserving his intellectual and physical powers in a wonderful degree, he died in Savannah on the 9th of January, 1805,[1] honored by the community as an accomplished gentleman, an influential citizen, a skillful physician, and a sterling patriot.

To the refined taste and liberality of his grandson, the late George Wymberley Jones De Renne, M. D.,

[1] His will was probated on the 19th of February, 1807, and remains of file in the office of the Ordinary of Chatham County, in Savannah.

of Savannah, a gentleman of broad education (enriched by study, travel, and observation), of large wealth, exquisite culture, and thoroughly imbued with a love for Georgia and all her traditions, are we indebted, among other literary legacies, for the series of *Wormsloe Quartos*, esteemed alike for their intrinsic value, admirable manufacture, and extreme rarity.

Since his death his widow — manifesting like generous interest in everything appertaining to the early history of Georgia, and as a tribute to the memory of her husband — has borne the charge of two other beautiful and expensive Wormsloe Quartos, edited by the writer, one entitled *Acts passed by the General Assembly of the Colony of Georgia*, 1755 *to* 1774. *Now first printed. Wormsloe. MDCCCLXXXI*; and the other, *A Journal of the Transactions of the Trustees for establishing the Colony of Georgia in America, by the R^t^ Honble John, Earl of Egmont, Viscount Perceval of Canturk, Baron Perceval of Burton, one of his Majesty's Most Privy Council in the Kingdom of Ireland, and first President of the Board of Trustees of the Colony of Georgia. Now first printed. Wormsloe. MDCCCLXXXVI.* In each case the edition was limited to forty-nine copies.

EDWARD LANGWORTHY.

This member of the Continental Congress was born in Savannah, Georgia, of obscure parentage. Left an orphan at a tender age, he was indebted for his maintenance and education to that charitable institution founded and long supported by the Reverend George Whitefield, and known as the Bethesda Orphan House. At a subsequent period he became a teacher in that school. His earliest public appearance, so far as we can ascertain, was as one of the signers of a card which was published in the *Georgia Gazette*, on the 7th of September, 1774, criticising certain patriotic resolutions adopted at a convocation of citizens held on the 10th of the preceding month, and protesting against their being accepted as reflecting the sentiments of a majority of the inhabitants of Georgia. In that card he appears as in full sympathy with the Royalists in the Province. That his political views underwent a sudden and violent change may be fairly inferred from the fact that in the following year he became the efficient Secretary of the Republican Council of Safety. In 1777 he was elected a delegate from Georgia to the Continental Congress. A similar honor was conferred upon him during the following year, when, with his confrères George Walton and Edward Telfair, he signed the Articles of Confederation. He at one time held the position of Justice of the Peace for the County of Chatham.

Not very long after the conclusion of peace between Great Britain and the United Colonies, he removed from Savannah and located in Maryland. He there formed the design of writing a history of Georgia. Of fair attainments, and possessing a personal acquaintance with many of the prominent persons and leading events appertaining to Georgia during the latter half of the eighteenth century, he was at least measurably qualified for the task. He seems to have addressed himself with energy to the collection of materials requisite for the undertaking. It would appear, from a prospectus printed in the *Georgia Gazette*, that the history was actually written, and that the manuscript was ready to be rendered into type. One of his letters lies before us, dated at Elkton, Maryland, March 1, 1791, and addressed to Seaborn Jones, Esq., Augusta, Georgia, in which Mr. Langworthy says: "Inclosed you will receive a Subscription Paper for 'A Political History of the State of Georgia,' &c., for which I must request you to take in subscriptions, and I flatter myself you will succeed therein, as the design is a well-meant attempt to rescue the patriotic exertions of our Countrymen from Oblivion and the Misrepresentation of some Writers of American History.

"What monies you will receive on this occasion you will please to pay to Mr. James Johnston, Printer at Savannah, whose receipt will be your discharge."

Suitable encouragement, however, not having been obtained, the contemplated publication was never made. Mr. Langworthy died at Elkton, Maryland, near the close of the last century, and all efforts to recover both his manuscript and the supporting documents which he had amassed have thus far proved abortive.

LACHLAN McINTOSH.

To the Continental Army Georgia furnished only two officers who attained the rank of Brigadier-General. They were Lachlan McIntosh and Samuel Elbert. Both were excellent soldiers, sterling patriots, and influential citizens. Their services, alike in peace and in war, were held in high repute. It is of the former of them that we would speak.

Born near Raits, in Badenoch, Scotland, on the 17th of March, 1725, when only eleven years of age he accompanied his father, John More McIntosh, to Georgia. Commissioned by the Trustees for the establishment of the Colony of Georgia in America, Lieutenant Hugh MacKay, in 1735, accepted and enrolled at Inverness one hundred and thirty Highlanders, with fifty women and children. The men were of good character, and were selected for their military qualities. Many of them came from the Glen of Stralbdean, and were commanded by officers most respectably connected in the Highlands. John More McIntosh was the head of the Borlam branch of the clan McIntosh. Conveyed on board the *Prince of Wales*, Captain George Dunbar, these sturdy immigrants set sail for Georgia on the 18th of October, 1735, and entered the mouth of the Savannah River early in the following January. Shortly afterwards, accompanied by a minister of their own selection, — the Reverend John McLeod, a native of the Isle of Skye, — these Highlanders were transported in periaguas to the southward. Ascending the Alatamaha River to a point on the left bank of that stream about sixteen miles above St. Simon's Island, they there landed, and formed a permanent settlement which they named "New Inverness." Here they erected a fort, mounted four pieces of cannon, built a guard-house, a store, and a chapel, and constructed dwellings for their accommodation. These Scots were a brave, hardy race,—just the men to occupy this advanced post and defend the southern confines of the Colony. "In their plaids, and with their broadswords, targets, and firearms, they presented a most manly appearance." Most valuable was the military service rendered by these Highlanders during the wars between the Georgia colonists and the Spaniards in Florida. John More McIntosh was appointed by Oglethorpe commandant of New Inverness. When, in 1740, General Oglethorpe invaded Florida and attempted the reduction of St. Augustine, he was accompanied by Captain McIntosh and his Highlanders. Unfortunately, although they "fought like lions," and "made such havoc with their broadswords as the Spaniards cannot easily forget," they were surprised and dispersed with great loss at Fort Moosa. Captain McIntosh was captured and sent as a prisoner to Spain, where he was detained for several years. When released, he returned to Georgia enfeebled in constitution. He did not long survive the privations which he had endured.

Lachlan McIntosh, while still a lad, was enrolled by General Oglethorpe as a cadet in his regiment. Amid the distractions of the period, and remembering the limited means then afforded for acquiring an education in Georgia, as may be well imagined, the subject of this sketch enjoyed but small opportunity for consecutive study and intellectual improvement. And yet we are told that his mother was most earnest in imparting the rudiments of an English education; and that, under the patronage of General Oglethorpe, young McIntosh was instructed in mathematics, and in other branches of knowledge deemed specially necessary for a military training.

At the age of seventeen he went to Charles-Town, and was there so fortunate as to enlist the friendly aid of the Honorable Henry Laurens, and to secure employment in his counting room. So kind was that gentleman to him, that during his residence in that city he remained an inmate of his family. Association with one so polite, refined, and accomplished, proved of great benefit to young McIntosh, and materially conduced to his intellectual and social advancement. At this period of his life he is described as "exhibiting a fine, manly appearance, and possessing a calm, firm temper."

Seemingly wearied with commercial engagements, when scarcely of age he took leave of his distinguished friend and patron and returned to his home at New Inverness, where he married, and adopted the calling of a surveyor. There was ample field for employment, and good opportunity for the selection of valuable lands lying between the Alatamaha and the river St. Mary. Of these chances McIntosh availed himself, quickly securing a comfortable livelihood, and acquiring the promise of a considerable fortune. It was while thus engaged that the subject of this sketch was called upon to declare his sympathies in the discussion which was daily becoming more violent between the Rebel element in the Province and the adherents to the Crown. Manifestly there was no hesitation on his part in casting his lot with the Revolutionists.

Early in January, 1775, a District Congress was held by the inhabitants of St. Andrew's Parish, at which a series of manly resolutions — embodying the views of a large number of the most influential citizens of the Alatamaha settlements — was adopted with much enthusiasm. The first of these resolutions expressed the unqualified approval by the members of that Congress of "the unparalleled moderation, the decent but firm and manly conduct of the loyal and brave people of Boston and Massachusetts Bay" in their efforts to preserve their liberties; their acquiescence in and sanction of "all the resolutions of the Grand American Congress;" and their "cheerful accession to the association entered into by them as the wisest and most moderate measure that could be adopted." The second resolution, after condemning the closing of the land offices to the great detriment of colonial growth and the injury of the industrious poor, declared that every "encouragement should be given to the indigent of every nation by every generous American." The third criticised severely ministerial mandates which prohibited Colonial Assemblies from passing such laws as the exigencies of their respective Provinces required. In the fourth, the practice of making colonial officers dependent upon Great Britain for the determination and payment of their salaries, thus rendering them "independent of the people who should support them according to their usefulness and behaviour," was heartily condemned. By the fifth, the Parish declared its "disapprobation and abhorrence of the unnatural practice of slavery in America," and its determination to urge the manumission of our slaves in this Colony upon the most safe and equitable footing for the masters and themselves." The last resolution provided for the election of delegates to represent the district in a Provincial Congress, and instructed them to urge the appointment of deputies from Georgia to the Continental Congress.

Appended to these resolutions, which among others were signed by Lachlan McIntosh, appeared the following Articles of Association: —

"Being persuaded that the salvation of the rights and liberties of America depend, under God, on the firm union of the inhabitants in the vigorous prosecution of the measures necessary for its safety, and convinced of the necessity of preventing the anarchy and confusion which attend the dissolution of the forces of government, we, the freemen, freeholders, and inhabitants of the Province of Georgia, being greatly alarmed at the avowed design of the ministry to raise a revenue in America, and shocked by the bloody scenes now acting in the Massachusetts Bay, do in the most solemn manner resolve never to become slaves; and do associate under all the ties of religion, honor, and love of country to adopt and endeavor to carry into execution whatever may be recommended by the Continental Congress, or resolved upon by our Provincial Convention that shall be appointed, for the purpose of preserving our Constitution and opposing the execution of the several arbitrary and oppressive acts of the British Parliament, until a reconciliation between Great Britain and America on constitutional principles, which we most ardently desire, can be obtained; and that we will in all things follow the advice of our General Committee, to be appointed, respecting the purposes aforesaid, the preservation of peace and good order, and the safety of individuals and private property."

It was in view of these and similar resolutions adopted by other parishes in Georgia, that Sir James Wright, in addressing the Earl of Dartmouth on the 13th of February, 1775, said: "Really, my Lord, a great many People have worked themselves up to such a pitch of political enthusiasm with respect to their ideas of Liberty and the powers of the British Parliament, and of their *right to resist* what they call unconstitutional laws, that I do not expect they will yet give up their pretensions."

In the important Provincial Congress which assembled in Savannah on the 4th of July, 1775, Lachlan McIntosh sat as a delegate from the Parish of St. Andrew, and sympathized fully in the conclusions of that body.

On the 7th of January, 1776, the battalion, which the Continental Congress on the 4th of the previous November ordered to be raised at the common charge of the United Provinces for the protection of Georgia, was organized by commissioning line officers for the eight companies which composed it, and by appointing Lachlan McIntosh as Colonel, Samuel Elbert as Lieutenant-Colonel, and Joseph Habersham as Major. From this time forward, and until American independence was conceded by the mother country, Lachlan McIntosh remained in the military service of the Confederated Provinces.

A question having arisen touching a possible conflict of authority between the Continental Congress and the Georgia Provincial Congress, or Council of Safety, in regard to the command of this battalion, — the enlistment of which upon a Continental establishment had been sanctioned and aided by the General Congress, — the matter was set at rest by a written declaration, signed by all the field and line officers of that organization, pledging themselves as soldiers and men of honor to obey all orders emanating from the Congresses or Councils of Safety of Georgia, where the same did not conflict with the "directions of the General Congress, or a committee thereof, or of any general or other officer by them appointed."

In forwarding a copy of this document to General George Washington, Commander-in-Chief of the American forces, Colonel McIntosh, on the 16th of February, 1776, furnished an interesting account of the population, resources, and dangers of the Province, requested general instructions as to the conduct of military affairs within the limits of the Colony, and asked to be informed how far his command was under the orders of the Provincial Congress, and what rank he and his officers should hold when acting with the militia.

In March, 1776, when Majors Maitland and Grant attempted the capture of the rice-laden vessels lying in the river opposite Savannah, Colonel McIntosh with three hundred men proceeded to Yamacraw Bluff, where he hastily threw up a breastwork and posted three four-pounder guns bearing upon the shipping. From this battery, for four hours he fired upon the enemy. Galled by canister and solid shot, supplemented by rifle balls from sharpshooters and by vessels ignited and turned adrift in the river, the British troops abandoned their attempt and resumed their station in Tybee Roads. This was the first passage-at-arms within the limits of Georgia between the "Sons of Liberty" and the King's soldiers. The Rubicon had been passed. Blood had been shed, and resistance to the death offered on the part of Georgians to English dominion. The patriotism displayed by the citizens of Savannah, and the manhood exhibited on this occasion in defense of their homes and property, merit high commendation. Apprehending another and a more serious demonstration, Colonel McIntosh detained his battalion in Savannah ready for action. Complying with a custom which had obtained when Georgia was ruled by Royal governors, Colonel McIntosh, when the Honorable Archibald Bulloch was elected President and Commander-in-Chief of Georgia, posted a sentinel at the door of his residence. To this his Excellency objected, with the remark, "I act for a free people in whom I have the most entire confidence, and I wish to avoid on all occasions the appearance of ostentation."

When, on the 10th of August, the Declaration of Independence was promulgated in Savannah by President Bulloch, Colonel McIntosh commanded the procession and fired the salutes.

Responding to the request of General Charles Lee, Jonathan Bryan, John Houstoun, and Colonel McIntosh — representing the Council of Safety of Georgia — waited upon that officer (then in command of the Southern Department) at Charlestown, and suggested a plan of operations by which it was hoped annoying banditti from Florida might be slain or dispersed, and the town of St. Augustine captured. Moved by the representations of this committee, and anxious to put a stop to the depredations upon the southern frontier of Georgia, General Lee resolved upon an expedition for the reduction of East Florida. In the movement then inaugurated Colonel McIntosh and his command participated, but it was not pressed beyond Sunbury. Want of preparation, the absence of necessary stores and transportation, and the recall of General Lee converted the whole affair into a miserable fiasco. Thereupon Colonel McIntosh, taking counsel of himself, made the best possible disposition of his command along the southern frontier of Georgia for its protection. Various skirmishes occurred in this direction, and the Province was kept in a state of constant alarm.

The General Assembly of Georgia resolved to add three battalions of infantry and a squadron of dragoons to the troops serving on the Continental establishment, to form them into a brigade, and to promote Colonel McIntosh to the rank of Brigadier-General and assign him to their command. Button Gwinnett had been a candidate for this position, and he was much embittered by McIntosh's success. When by the Council of Safety Mr. Gwinnett was elected President and Commander-in-Chief of Georgia until such time as a governor could be appointed under the provisions of the Constitution recently adopted, that gentleman, quick in action, brave and ambitious, sought to signalize his administration by an expedition against Florida. The expectation of retaliation was pleasing to the public; and President Gwinnett hoped, by a quick descent, to take the Floridians unawares and win an easy victory.

Intent upon mortifying McIntosh, who, as the ranking military officer of Georgia, was entitled to command the troops detailed for the movement, he set him aside, assigned subordinates to special columns, and determined himself to assume personal conduct and control of the expedition. This of course widened the breach between those gentlemen. As the story of this ill-timed and disastrous expedition has already been fully told in the sketch of Button Gwinnett, we refrain from repeating it in this connection.

In the political contest which occurred between Button Gwinnett and John Adam Treutlen, during the session of the Legislature in May, 1777, for the gubernatorial chair, the latter was successful. Treutlen's cause had been warmly espoused by McIntosh, who was open and violent in his denunciations of Gwinnett. The quarrel between these quick-tempered and brave men culminated in a duel, fought on the morning of the 16th of May, 1777, within the present limits of the city of Savannah. The weapons used were pistols, and the principals were posted at the short distance of only four paces. At the first discharge both were struck. Gwinnett's thigh was shattered, and he sank upon the ground. When asked if he desired to exchange another shot, he responded, "Yes, if I should be helped up." The seconds, however, intervened, and Gwinnett was borne from the field. The weather was very hot. Mortification quickly ensued, and Gwinnett expired on the fourth day after receiving his mortal hurt. McIntosh was confined to his couch for some time. Gwinnett's death created much excitement. Dr. Lyman Hall — a warm personal friend of the deceased, and one of his executors — and other prominent gentlemen brought the matter to the notice of the Legislature, and accused the officers of the law of a neglect of duty in not arresting McIntosh and binding him over to answer to a charge of murder. Informed of what was transpiring, the General, as soon as his wound would permit, surrendered himself to Judge Glen, entered into bond for his appearance, was indicted, tried, and acquitted. Even this determination of the matter did not allay the animosity of Gwinnett's friends, who, angered at the death of their leader, endeavored to impair the influence of McIntosh, and to fetter his usefulness in the public service. Moved by the circumstances, invoking the intervention of his friend, the Honorable Henry Laurens, and finally securing an order[1] from the Continental Congress, General McIntosh — surrendering his command in Georgia, and taking with him as his deputy adjutant-general his son, Captain Lachlan McIntosh, and as his brigade major his young friend, Captain John Berrien — reported at Washington's headquarters for assignment to another field of duty. For some time he was placed in advance of the central army, and was actively engaged in watching the movements of General Howe's forces, then concentrated in Philadelphia. Subsequently he was entrusted with the command of the western districts of Virginia and Pennsylvania. So soon as measures had been fully concerted between Count D'Estaing and General Benjamin Lincoln for the repossession of Savannah and Southern Georgia, then held by the British troops under General Prevost, anxious to participate in this important movement, General McIntosh, who had then completed his

[1] Dated August 1, 1777.

arrangements for an attack upon Detroit, applied for permission to return to Georgia. Sympathizing in the propriety of this wish on the part of his lieutenant, General Washington signified his approval, and gave to General McIntosh a letter addressed to the Continental Congress, in which, under date of May 11, 1779, he says: "Brigadier-General McIntosh will have the honor of delivering you this. The war in Georgia, being the State to which he belongs, makes him desirous of serving in the Southern army. I know not whether the arrangements Congress have in contemplation may make it convenient to employ him there: but I take the liberty to recommend him as a gentleman whose knowledge of service and of the country promises to make him useful. I beg leave to add, that General McIntosh's conduct, while he acted immediately under my observation, was such as to acquire my esteem and confidence, and I have had no reason since to alter my good opinion of him."

His application being sanctioned by the Continental Congress, General McIntosh proceeded to Charlestown, where he reported to General Benjamin Lincoln, then in command of the Southern Department. By that officer he was assigned to the command of the Continental forces in Georgia, and his headquarters were, for the time being, established at Augusta. It was from this point, in association with Count Pulaski, that General McIntosh, early in September, 1779, moved upon Savannah, reaching its vicinity in advance of the army under General Lincoln, occupying a position between that town and Great Ogeechee Ferry, and there awaiting the concentration of the allied troops. It lies not within the compass of this sketch to recount the incidents connected with the siege of Savannah.[1] Suffice it to say that General McIntosh, as second in command of the American forces, actively participated in the siege, and led one of the columns of assault on the Spring Hill redoubt, on the bloody and disastrous morning of the 9th of October, 1779. In the conduct of all operations committed to his guidance he exhibited a courage and an ability worthy of every commendation. His position was peculiarly trying, for his wife and family were within the city lines, and were for weeks exposed to the fury of the fire of the investing batteries.

When the siege was raised, the French troops — betaking themselves to their fleet — departed; and the American forces under General Lincoln retreated upon Charlestown, where, after a protracted and gallant defense, they were compelled to surrender to General Clinton. Among the general officers captured on that occasion was Brigadier-General Lachlan McIntosh. When released, he retired with his family to Virginia; from that time forward, and until the successful termination of the war, participating but little in military affairs. His companions in arms, when they were made acquainted with his purpose to establish his temporary home in Virginia, united in a complimentary communication to Governor Jefferson, commending General McIntosh to the particular notice of that State, and requesting in his behalf such allowance of lands and other emoluments as were given for the encouragement and reward of efficient officers belonging to the Virginia line.

[1] For a full account, see Jones's *History of Georgia*, vol. ii. pp. 375–416. Boston: Houghton, Mifflin & Co. 1883.

Upon his return to Georgia in 1779, after an absence of some two years, General McIntosh hoped that time had healed all wounds, and that he would be permitted, without jealousy or opposition, to devote his time and energies to the defense of his home and people. In this pleasing anticipation he was disappointed. On the 30th of November, 1779, a letter, purporting to be signed by William Glascock, Speaker of the House of Representatives, was transmitted by George Walton, then Governor of Georgia, to the President of the Continental Congress, assuring that body of the dissatisfaction experienced by the people of Georgia at the assignment of General McIntosh to the command of the military in that State, and earnestly suggesting that "some distant field for the exercise of his abilities" should be selected. So thoroughly did this communication, supported by the representations of General McIntosh's enemies, poison the minds of the members of the Continental Congress that they resolved, on the 15th of February, 1780, to "dispense with the services of Brigadier-General McIntosh until the further order of Congress."

Upon inquiry, this letter proved to be an utter forgery; and, after a review of the whole affair, the Legislature of Georgia "resolved that General McIntosh be informed that this House does entertain an abhorrence of all such injurious attempts made use of, as appears by the papers laid before them, to injure the character of an officer and citizen of this State who merits the attention of the Legislature for his early, decided, and persevering efforts in the defense of America; of which virtue this House has the highest sense."

Upon the evacuation of Savannah by General Alured Clarke and the King's forces in the summer of 1782, General McIntosh returned with his family to Georgia, and, from that time until his death on the 20th of February, 1806, continued to reside in that town and its vicinity. In 1784 he was complimented with a seat in the Continental Congress. Of the important commission charged with the settlement of the boundary between Georgia and South Carolina he was a member. He also represented Georgia in the accommodation of disputes with the Creek and Cherokee nations.

With the exception of these occasional and limited public employments, General McIntosh passed the remainder of his days in retirement. Although small his fortune, he was rich in the esteem, the friendship, and the gratitude of his fellow-citizens.

He was for years the President of the Georgia Branch of the Society of the Cincinnati. Upon the occasion of President Washington's visit to Savannah in May, 1791, he was attended by General McIntosh when he inspected the lines constructed by the British in 1779 for the defense of Savannah, and the approaches and batteries then made by the Allied Army. Having himself participated in the siege and in the assault of the 9th of October, General McIntosh was able to convey to the President full information touching the whole affair. The earth mounds covering the slain, the lines of circumvallation, the sand parapets and gun chambers, had not then yielded to the influences of time and an encroaching population. The scars of the siege were still upon the bosom of the plain, and some of the houses within the limits of the city bore the marks of the lethal missiles which were then hurled. About him stood those who had passed through that baptism of fire. The President exhibited a deep interest in everything he then saw and heard.

The writer of the memoir which appears in the third volume of "The National Portrait Gallery of Distinguished Americans" describes General McIntosh as being five feet eleven inches tall, "of athletic form and great activity." While a lad at New Inverness, there was not an Indian in the neighborhood who could compete with him in fleetness of foot; and when twenty-five years of age, a friend spoke of him as "the handsomest man he had ever seen." A county in Southern Georgia perpetuates the name of the McIntosh family, which, since its settlement upon the Alatamaha, has in four wars given brave and distinguished members to the military service of colony, commonwealth, and nation.[1]

[1] General McIntosh's will was probated in Chatham County, Georgia, on the 5th of May, 1806, and is now of file in the Ordinary's Office in Savannah.

WILLIAM PIERCE.

It is claimed by respectable authority that this gentleman was born in Georgia about 1740. Of his early life we find no mention beyond the fact that his education was liberal, and that his pursuits were mercantile in their character. His first distinction was won in arms as an aide-de-camp to General Nathanael Greene, whose friendship and confidence he appears to have enjoyed to the fullest extent. For his meritorious conduct at the battle of Eutaws he was complimented by the American Congress and presented with a sword. In the Continental service he rose to the grade of major.

Upon the conclusion of the war of the Revolution Major Pierce resumed his residence in Savannah, where he became the head of the mercantile house of William Pierce & Co. Chancing upon misfortune, that firm went into liquidation in 1788. During the years 1786 and 1787 he was a Delegate from Georgia to the Continental Congress. He had previously represented the County of Chatham in the State Legislature.

On the 10th of February, 1787, in association with William Few, Abram Baldwin, George Walton, William Houstoun, and Nathaniel Pendleton, he was appointed a deputy from Georgia to the Philadelphia Convention called for the purpose of revising the Federal Constitution. He took his seat in that Convention on the 31st of May, and participated in the deliberations. He was not present when the Constitution finally formulated was signed. His impressions of the labors and conclusions of the Convention are given *in extenso* in a well-considered and very interesting letter, dated in New York city on the 28th of September, 1787, and addressed by him to St. George Tucker, Esquire. The full text of this important communication may be found in the *Georgia Gazette* of March 20, 1788.

That letter inclosed to Mr. Tucker a copy of the Constitution. "You will," writes Major Pierce, "probably be surprised at not finding my name affixed to it; and will no doubt be desirous of having a reason for it. Know then, Sir, that I was absent in New York on a piece of business so necessary that it became unavoidable. I approve of its principles, and would have signed it with all my heart had I been present. To say, however, that I consider it as perfect would be to make an acknowledgment immediately opposed to my judgment. Perhaps it is the only one which will suit our present situation. The wisdom of the Convention was equal to something greater; but a variety of local circumstances, the inequality of States, and the dissonant interests of the different parts of the Union made it impossible to give it any other shape or form."

The writer then passes the salient features of the Constitution in a review worthy of careful consideration, which we would gladly here reproduce did the limits of this sketch permit. He was an earnest advocate of an election by the people of the members of the House of Representatives, and by the States of the Senators, whose terms of service he preferred to limit to three years.

Major Pierce died in the city of Savannah, Georgia,

on the 10th of December, 1789, and the following tribute to his memory is reproduced from the contemporary columns of the *Georgia Gazette*: —

"To speak of the dead is no uncommon thing: however, a friend cannot refrain from paying the last tribute to the manes of MAJOR WILLIAM PIERCE, who died last Thursday week [December 10, 1789] universally regretted. He, at an early period of the contest between America and Great Britain, took a decided part in favour of his country, which he loved to his last moments: for we may say when the hand of Death was over him he was a candidate to become its servant. He was particularly noticed by that gallant officer Gen. Greene, who honoured him with his *friendship and most secret confidence.* Congress in respect to his services at the battle of the *Eutaws* made him a compliment of an elegant *Sword* as a token of their approbation of his conduct. He had the honour to represent Chatham County in the General Assembly; and was sent as a Delegate from this State to Congress at a time when deliberation and great judgment were necessary; which duties he discharged to the satisfaction of his *Country.*

"Though born with a delicate constitution, he had till lately enjoyed a firm, uninterrupted state of health, which however was, from the fatigues of the war, diversities of climes and elements, at length undermined and destroyed: His manners polite and obliging, his reasonings precise, his diction[1] perspicuous and eloquent: His love of truth was not tainted by the desire of popularity, nor his modesty impaired by the favours of those in power; for he was of no *party*, but the gen-

[1] See his oration delivered on the 4th July.

eral good of his country; His way of thinking had preserved him from the pursuits of selfishness and *sordid intrigues:* his character appeared worthy of the *favours of Fortune;* but alas! he stood the hardest tests of misfortune: a sincere, and occasionally an active friend; always *an agreeable companion.* The Society of the Cincinnati honoured him as their Vice President, and by whom he was attended as mourners to the tomb. An affectionate and endearing husband, a kind master, and all that was worth possessing in a domestick situation. He supported a lingering disease, and beheld the slow approaches of Death with philosophical calmness and serenity; and I am told by a friend who visited him at that *solemn period*, when he took leave of his wife and friends his soul seemed, as it were, already received in the blissful mansions of the blessed — to make use of his own words, which were the last he uttered, 'Farewell! farewell all! Now dies the happy man.'"[1]

Upon the 4th of July, 1789, when the anniversary of American Independence was celebrated by the Georgia Society of the Cincinnati, at Hamilton's Long Room in Savannah, and the oration was pronounced by Major Pierce, the following officers were elected: —

Major-General Anthony Wayne, President.
Major William Pierce, Vice-President.
Major John Habersham, Secretary.
Colonel Richard Wylly, Treasurer.
John Peter Ward, Esqr., Assistant Secretary.
Edward Lloyd, Esqr., Assistant Treasurer.

At the "elegant dinner" which crowned a day of "great harmony and conviviality" the following toasts were drank: —

[1] The *Georgia Gazette* [No. 361], Thursday, December 24, 1789.

"1. The President-General of the Society and of the Union.

2. The respective State Societies.

3. Prosperity and Happiness to our dear Country.

4. The People.

5. Agriculture and Commerce.

6. The Legislature of the Union; — wisdom, unanimity, and a happy operation to their measures.

7. Peace and Harmony.

8. The King of France, and the Officers of his Army who assisted in establishing the American Independence.

9. The Governor and State of Georgia.

10. The Memory of our departed Brethren.

11. The Republicks of the World, where law and not the will of despots rules.

12. May Policy dictate a just Reward for Publick Service.

13. May North Carolina and Rhode Island by a speedy Adoption of the Federal Constitution complete the Number of the Thirteen United States."

SAMUEL STIRK.

Mr. Stirk is believed to have been a native of Savannah, Georgia. He there resided and was a practitioner of law when he first attracted public notice.

Of the Executive Council chosen in 1777 — when John Adam Treutlen, defeating Button Gwinnett, was elected first Republican Governor of Georgia — Benjamin Andrew was complimented with the Presidency, and Samuel Stirk was appointed Clerk.

By the Assembly convened in Augusta he was, on the 16th of August, 1781, elected a Delegate from Georgia to the Continental Congress. By the same Legislature he was honored with the position of Attorney-General of Georgia, and to this office he was reelected in January, 1783. Simultaneously with this latter appointment, he was named as a Commissioner on the part of the State to negotiate with Governor Patrick Tonyn, of East Florida, for the accommodation of all differences and the prevention of further disturbances along the line of the river St. Mary.

Among the Justices of Chatham County his name appears in 1786, and also in 1789. During the last-mentioned year he was President of the Board of Wardens of Savannah.

In 1778 and 1779 he was in the military service of the State and Confederation; and, with the rank of Lieutenant-Colonel, participated in the ill-starred expedition launched by President Gwinnett against East Florida.

EDWARD TELFAIR.

This gentleman, distinguished alike for his attractive social qualities, admirable business methods, integrity, financial ability, and statesmanlike conduct, was a native of Scotland. He was born in 1735 on the farm of Town Head, the ancestral estate of the Telfairs, which has since passed into the ownership of the Earl of Selkirk. Having received his English education at the grammar school of Kirkcudbright, he subsequently applied himself to the acquisition of a thorough commercial training, and at the age of twenty-three coming to America as the representative of a business house, resided for some time in Virginia. He afterwards removed to Halifax, North Carolina, and subsequently, in 1766, settled in Savannah, Georgia.[1] By energy, thrift, fair dealing, and enterprise, he soon established a lucrative business in what was then the commercial metropolis of the Province. Deeply immersed in trade was he when the disagreements between the American Colonies and the mother country began to assume decided and alarming proportions. That he did not long hesitate in choosing sides upon the momentous questions which then agitated the public mind may be fairly inferred, because, as early as the

[1] See Johnson's *Traditions and Reminiscences, chiefly of the Revolution in the South*, p. 200. Charleston, S. C., 1851.

27th of July, 1774, we find him a member of two committees raised by the Republican party in Georgia,—one to assure the other American Colonies of the rebel sentiments of the Province, and of its determination to share the common lot in the effort to win independence from British rule; and the other to solicit and forward supplies for the relief of the suffering patriots in Boston.

As a Delegate elected by the liberty-seeking citizens of Savannah on the 8th of December in the same year, he participated in the deliberations of the Provincial Congress which assembled on the 18th of the following January.

In association with Dr. Noble W. Jones, Joseph Habersham, and others,—most of them members of the Council of Safety and all zealous in the cause of American freedom,—he personally assisted in breaking open the public magazine in Savannah, and in removing therefrom a goodly quantity of the King's powder with which to supply the urgent needs of the Revolutionists.

On the 21st of June, 1775, he was elected a member of the Council of Safety; and, in the Provincial Congress which assembled in Savannah on the 4th of the following July, he appeared and took his seat as a Delegate from the "Town and District of Savannah." He was of the committee then selected to frame an address to his Excellency Governor Wright; was placed upon the "Committee of Intelligence;" and was constituted a member of another committee to present to the inhabitants of the town and district of Savannah the "Article of Association" adopted by the Congress. Before adjourning, this body, on the 11th of December, elected a new Council of Safety, and Mr. Telfair was named as one of its members.

Early in 1778 he was chosen a Delegate from Georgia to the Continental Congress. In the following July, together with George Walton and Edward Langworthy, he affixed his signature to the "Articles of Confederation." One leave of absence excepted, he remained a member of the Continental Congress until January, 1783. In May, 1785, he was complimented by another election to the old Congress, but it is believed that he did not resume his seat in obedience to this summons. While in Congress his services were specially valuable in the domain of finances. On the 15th of February, 1783, he was designated as an agent on the part of Georgia to settle the northern boundary of the Commonwealth. He also represented the State in consummating, at Augusta, during the same year, important treaties with the Cherokee and Creek Indians.

Three years afterwards he was honored with the Chief Magistracy of Georgia. His conduct in the discharge of this exalted trust was characterized by wisdom, dignity, and firmness. It required no little skill and discretion to avoid a threatened war with the Cherokees. In compelling the removal of the public records from Savannah to the seat of government, he encountered not only the protest but also the active opposition of many prominent parties. The measures, however, which he adopted to compass this proper transfer were so prompt and decisive that both the dignity of the Commonwealth and the majesty of the law were maintained. Much of his time and thought was bestowed upon the public finances, and in devising the best scheme for liberating Georgia from the annoying indebtedness which then oppressed her. It was during his administration that Georgia was called upon to mourn the demise of her adopted son, who, next to Washington, challenged the public confidence and esteem, — the great and good General Nathanael Greene. In obedience to his orders, reckless bands of runaway slaves, who, defying the laws, with arms in their hands, were plundering the plantations on the Lower Savannah, were thoroughly dispersed by the militia.

He was a member of the convention which ratified the Constitution of the United States.

On the 9th of November, 1789, Mr. Telfair was again called to the gubernatorial chair. He was the first chief magistrate elected and qualified under the new Constitution. It was his pleasure and privilege to welcome to his home in Augusta, which was then the capital of the State, President Washington, in May, 1791, and to extend every honor and courtesy which place and circumstance could contribute. On the departure of the General, he addressed to Governor Telfair the following courteous communication: —

"AUGUSTA, *20th May*, 1791.

"TO HIS EXCELLENCY EDWARD TELFAIR,

Governor of Georgia:

"SIR, — Obeying the impulse of a heartfelt gratitude, I express with particular pleasure my sense of obligations which your Excellency's goodness and the kind regard of your citizens have conferred upon me. I shall always retain a most pleasing remembrance of the polite and hospitable attentions which I have received in my tour through the State of Georgia, and during my stay at the residence of your government.

"The manner in which you are pleased to recognize my public services, and to regard my private felicity, excites my sensibility and claims my grateful acknowledgments. Your Excellency will do justice to the sentiments which influence my wishes by believing that they are sincerely offered for your personal happiness and the prosperity of the State over which you preside.

"George Washington."

The hospitality extended by Governor Telfair, on this occasion, to his distinguished guest at his home on the outskirts of Augusta, called *The Grove*, was generous and refined to the last degree.

Without specifying the particular duties which claimed Governor Telfair's attention as the chief magistrate of Georgia, it may be stated that to the performance of his public duties he brought broad experience, business capacity of a high order, a singleness of purpose, and a devotion to duty which made his administration of the affairs of state prompt, direct, and effective.

Upon the expiration of his gubernatorial labors he returned to his home in Savannah, where the last years of his life were given to the careful conduct of his extensive private business, to dispensing hospitality, and to participating in, and presiding over, convocations of his fellow-citizens on important occasions.

In this city he died on the 19th of September, 1807, and was buried with every honor which public esteem and private friendship could extend.

Among the members from Georgia of the Continental Congress Governor Telfair was perhaps possessed of the greatest wealth. Although during the war of the Revolution he encountered considerable mutation in fortune, and at one time with his family sought refuge in Fredericktown, Maryland, upon the return of peace he quickly recovered his losses and added largely to his former possessions.

Considering the place and the period, Governor Telfair's commercial operations were very successful and extensive. He maintained good credit in, and important business connections with, the West Indies, Charlestown, Philadelphia, New York, Newport, Liverpool, London, etc. Dealing largely in rice, lumber, cotton, indigo, and other staple commodities, he operated on his own account and sold upon commission. As the owner of sawmills judiciously located, and of several valuable plantations well equipped with negroes, animals, and agricultural implements, his income — aside from that derived from his commercial business — was generous. A capital financier, he became one of the richest men of his day and generation in Georgia; and the estate which he accumulated — properly husbanded and judiciously administered by his daughters — has recently been dispensed in public charities of the most useful and abundant character. Prominent among them may be mentioned Hodgson Hall — the home of the Georgia Historical Society — and the Telfair Academy of Arts and Sciences. In passing upon and sustaining the charitable bequests contained in the will of Miss Telfair, when their validity was questioned in the courts, Mr. Justice Bradley observed: "It is a laudable ambition to wish to transmit one's name to posterity by deeds of beneficence. The millionaire who leaves the world without doing anything for the benefit of society, or for the advancement of science, morality, or civilization, turns to dust and is forgotten; but he who employs a princely fortune in founding institutions for the alleviation of suffering or the elevation of his race erects a monument more noble, and generally more effective to preserve his name, than the Pyramids. Thousands of the wealthy and the noble in the early days of English civilization are deservedly forgotten; but the founders of colleges in Oxford and Cambridge will be borne on the grateful memories of Englishmen as long as their empire lasts. Harvard and Yale in our own country are pertinent examples of this truth."

In the history of testaments Georgia has never known charitable bequests of such magnitude and liberal scope as those passing under the wills of the daughters of Governor Telfair,[1] distributing the large estate which in great measure was accumulated and transmitted by him. Not only by these prominent charities, but also in the records of the period, and by a county named in his honor, is his memory worthily perpetuated.

[1] His will was probated in Chatham County on the 4th of January, 1808, and is now of file in the Ordinary's Office in Savannah.

GEORGE WALTON.

It was a remark of D'Alembert that high office resembles a pyramid, the summit of which can be reached only by reptiles and eagles.

We recall no citizen of Georgia who, during a life extending over little more than half a century, acquired loftier or more numerous honors within the gift of the Commonwealth than the Honorable George Walton. In the attainment, enjoyment, and execution of the political and judicial trusts committed to his keeping, no slime of the serpent besmirched his pathway. In the discharge of the duties devolved upon him he was fearless, conscientious, and capable. In all stations he fulfilled every legitimate expectation. Without the adjuvatives of birth, education, and fortune, he won and maintained his right to preferment by conscientious endeavor, consecutive study, tireless industry, and unquestioned ability. His life, labors, and success afford brilliant illustration of what, in this democratic country, may be achieved by honesty of purpose, natural talent, courageous action, earnest effort, and inflexible will.

Born in Prince Edward County, Virginia, in 1749, and becoming an orphan at a tender age, he passed under the care of a guardian who, as the family tradition runs, unwilling to assume the burden of his custody and education, apprenticed him to a carpenter. The industry and fidelity of the lad were commendable, and his desire for intellectual improvement attracted the notice both of employer and companions. Unable, during the day, to give any attention to his books, and too poor to afford the luxury of a lamp, he read them nightly by the light of fat fagots which he collected and husbanded for that purpose. Intent upon his studies, he refrained from those nocturnal sports which too often lead the young and inexperienced into dissipation, idleness, and sometimes ruin. By judicious use of his evening hours he made, under the circumstances, rapid advancement in knowledge; eagerly perusing all good books which could be borrowed from friends and neighbors.

So favorably impressed was the master with the character, intelligence, and ambition of his apprentice that long before his articles were concluded he relieved him from their obligation, and permitted him to retain the fruits of his daily industry. Thus young Walton accumulated some money, which enabled him, when about twenty years of age, to leave Virginia and seek new fortunes in Savannah.

Arriving at this little commercial metropolis of the Colony of Georgia, he resolved to become a lawyer. Henry Young, Esq., received him into his office, and gave him the benefit of his library and of his instruction. After suitable preparation he was called to the bar, and at once entered with zeal upon the practice of the profession of his choice. That success early attended upon his efforts may be fairly admitted; for we have before us an opinion given by him to Edward Telfair, Esq. — then a gentleman of influence and ample means, afterwards a member of the Continental Congress and a Governor of Georgia — upon a question of considerable moment. This opinion was furnished in 1774, and his employment by so prominent a merchant as Mr. Telfair speaks well for the standing of the young attorney in the community.

In 1777 he married Dorothy Camber, — young and fair, — to whom he was devotedly attached, and from whom, during the progress of the war of the Revolution, he for some time suffered painful separation.

The passage of the Boston Port Bill, the first step in a system of coercive measures adopted by the British ministry; — of a second act, which provided that the Provincial Council of Massachusetts — previously elected by the representative assembly in accordance with charter privileges — should thereafter be appointed by the Crown; that the Royal Governor should be invested with the power of nominating and removing judges, sheriffs, and other executive officers whose functions possessed the slightest importance; that jurymen, hitherto selected by the freeholders and citizens of the several towns, should in future be nominated and summoned by the sheriffs; that no town-meetings of the inhabitants should be convoked without permission in writing from the Royal Governor, and that no business should then be discussed other than the matters specified and approved in the Governor's license; — and of a third act, which empowered the Governor of the Province, if he saw fit, to commit any parties indicted for murder or charged with capital offenses, for trial, either to another Colony or to Great Britain, aroused the opposition of liberal statesmen in England, and was justly regarded in America as forming a complete system of tyranny. By the first, exclaimed the organs of popular opinion in the Colonies, thousands of innocent persons are, by the act of a few individuals, robbed of their livelihood; by the second, chartered liberties are annihilated; and by the third, lives may be destroyed with impunity. The passage of the Quebec Bill also enhanced the general indignation.

A knowledge of this legislation and an apprehension of its pernicious influence inflamed the minds of the patriots in South Carolina and Georgia, and induced them to give early and decided expression to their views of condemnation and opposition.

Responding to a public call, a respectable number of the freeholders and inhabitants of the Province assembled at the Watch House, in Savannah, on the 27th of July, 1774. After an animated discussion, a committee was raised, of which George Walton was a member, to prepare resolutions — similar to those adopted by the Northern Colonies — declaratory of Georgia's condemnation of the oppressive measures inaugurated by Parliament. That there might be an expression of opinion from some of the more distant parishes, — unrepresented in this convocation, — the meeting "stood adjourned" until the 10th of the following August.

Alarmed at the drift of events, Governor Wright convened his Council and consulted as to the best method of checking proceedings which he denounced as unjustifiable and revolutionary. As a result of the conference, Sir James issued a proclamation pronouncing the purposed assemblage "unconstitutional, illegal, and punishable by law," and warned all loyal subjects of his Majesty to refrain from participating therein. In direct opposition to the wish of his Excellency, and in utter disregard of his proclamation, a large meeting of the inhabitants of the Province was held at Tondee's Tavern, in Savannah, at the time designated. Resolutions, framed by the committee selected at the previous assemblage, were unanimously adopted, claiming that as protection and allegiance were reciprocal and, under the British Constitution, correlative terms, his Majesty's subjects in America had a clear and indisputable right to petition the Throne upon every emergency; condemning Parliamentary legislation with regard to the port of Boston, the abolition of the Charter of Massachusetts Bay, the attempt to tax without representation, and the effort to deprive any colonist of the privilege of trial by his peers from the vicinage; promising coöperation with sister American Colonies in all constitutional measures to obtain redress of American grievances, and in the effort to maintain the inestimable blessings derived from God and the Magna Charta; and appointing a committee of conference with full powers, and also a special committee to solicit, receive, and forward subscriptions and supplies for the suffering poor in Boston. With the preparation and support of these patriotic and comprehensive resolutions George Walton was earnestly and prominently connected.

As might be well imagined, the effect of this convention, and of the adoption of these resolutions, was to confirm the division of sentiment in Georgia upon the political questions of the day. The Royal party was strong and alert, while the "Liberty Boys" were intent upon acquiring the mastery and placing the Province fairly within the lists of the Revolutionists.

Although a motion to "send six deputies to the General Congress of the American Colonies" was entertained and pressed, it did not receive the sanction of the meeting of the 10th of August.

To the Republicans the position occupied by Georgia was distasteful and mortifying. From her isolated attitude, from her apparent indifference to the compact into which the American Colonies had entered, from the controlling influence of Governor Wright and his Council, and from the ban under which she was placed in the esteem of the Confederated Provinces by her failure to participate in the deliberations of and to be bound by the conclusions reached by the Continental Congress, they determined to liberate her at the earliest practicable moment.

St. John's Parish, impatient of the delay, acted upon her own responsibility; and, in advance of the Colony, sent Dr. Lyman Hall as a special Delegate to the Continental Congress.

On the 21st of June, 1775, a call was published, signed by Noble Wymberley Jones, Archibald Bulloch, John Houstoun, and George Walton, requesting the inhabitants of the town and district of Savannah to meet at the Liberty Pole on the following day, at ten o'clock in the forenoon, for the purpose of selecting a committee to bring about a union of Georgia with her sister Colonies in the cause of freedom. The alarming situation of affairs in America, and particularly in Georgia, was urged as a reason for punctual and full attendance.

At the appointed place and designated hour many were present; and a Council of Safety, consisting of William Ewen, William Le Conte, Joseph Clay, Basil Cooper, Samuel Elbert, William Young, Elisha Butler, Edward Telfair, John Glen, George Houstoun, George Walton, Joseph Habersham, Francis H.

Harris, John Smith, John Morel, and Seth John Cuthbert, was selected, with instructions to maintain an active correspondence with the Continental Congress, with Councils of Safety in other Provinces, and with committees raised in Georgia parishes. This business concluded, a number of gentlemen who had attended the meeting dined at Tondee's Tavern. A Union flag was hoisted upon the Liberty Pole, at the foot of which two field pieces were posted; thirteen patriotic toasts were drunk, each being responded to by discharges from the cannon and by martial music: and all this within sight and hearing of the Royal Governor and his Council. It was daily becoming more evident that the power of the King's party in Georgia was on the wane; that the period of doubt and hesitation was nearing an end; and that the Province would soon be prepared to link her fortunes with those of her twelve sisters. Meetings were called in all the parishes to commission Delegates to a Provincial Congress which was to assemble in Savannah on the 4th of July, 1775. The Colony was thoroughly aroused, and resolved upon decisive action. Even Governor Wright,— hitherto so hopeful of the future, and entertaining such high impression of the power of the Royal party, — in a letter to Lord Dartmouth, under date of the 17th of June, expressed the belief that the members of the approaching convention would not fail to "entirely approve of whatever might be determined upon by the Continental Congress."

Memorable in the political annals of Georgia were the proceedings of this Provincial Congress which convened in Savannah on the 4th of July, 1775. Every parish was represented, and the Delegates were fitting exponents of the intelligence, the dominant hopes, and the material interests of the communities from which they respectively came. This was Georgia's first secession convention. It placed the Province in active sympathy and confederated alliance with the twelve other American Colonies, practically annulled within her limits the operation of the objectionable acts of Parliament, questioned the supremacy of the Realm, and inaugurated measures calculated to accomplish the independence of the plantation and its erection into the dignity of a State. In all the political agitations and movements which antedated and led up to this important convocation, George Walton had borne a prominent part. He stood shoulder to shoulder with Archibald Bulloch, Noble Wymberley Jones, John Houstoun, the brothers Joseph and John Habersham, Jonathan Bryan, Joseph Clay, Edward Telfair, and others who were specially influential in dissipating the power of kingly rule.

This Congress perfected its organization by electing Archibald Bulloch president and George Walton secretary. While it lies not within the compass of this sketch to enumerate its proceedings, we may state in a general way that it proclaimed, in terms most emphatic, a just conception of the natural and constitutional rights which appertained to Georgians as citizens of the Colony and subjects of Great Britain; testified determined opposition to the late objectionable acts of Parliament; expressed admiration for the heroism of New England, and a stern resolve to share the fortunes of the sister Colonies; appointed Delegates to, and manifested a willingness to observe all orders promulgated by, the Continental Congress; professed unswerving loyalty to the principles of American liberty, and suggested measures deemed appropriate in the present perplexed condition of public affairs.

Mr. Walton was appointed upon the "Committee of Intelligence," and was also named as one of the members to present the "Article of Association," then adopted, to the inhabitants of the town and district of Savannah for signature by them. In association with the Rev. Dr. Zubly, Dr. Noble W. Jones, and William Young, he was commissioned to prepare and submit to the people of Georgia an address containing an account of the state of American affairs, and a narrative of the proceedings of this Provincial Congress. This address, which is said to have been framed by Mr. Walton, is a model of its kind.

In defiance of the protest of Governor Wright, Mr. Walton and his associates of the Council of Safety thoroughly purged the militia of the Loyal element which lurked in the ranks of its commissioned officers. By a resolution of this Provincial Congress, he was continued as a member of the Council of Safety; and of that body he was, in December, 1775, chosen president, with Edward Langworthy as secretary.

The onward march of the Revolution was rapid and irresistible. Everything passed quickly under the dominion of the patriots. Even the Royal Governor, escaping from confinement, fled the Province, and there was no one left to dispute the supremacy of the "Sons of Liberty."

Archibald Bulloch was elected president of the Provincial Congress which assembled in Savannah on the 20th of January, 1776. That sterling patriot, and John Houstoun, Lyman Hall, Button Gwinnett, and

George Walton were then chosen as Delegates to the Continental Congress. To them this official communication was addressed :

"GENTLEMEN, — Our remote situation from both the seat of power and arms keeps us so very ignorant of the counsels and ultimate designs of the Congress and of the transactions in the field, that we shall decline giving any particular instructions other than strongly to recommend it to you that you never lose sight of the Province ; the Indians, both south and northwestwardly upon our backs ; the fortified town of St. Augustine, made a continual rendezvous for soldiers in our very neighborhood ; together with our blacks and Tories with us : let these weighty truths be the powerful arguments for support. At the same time we also recommend it to you always to keep in view the general utility, remembering that the great and righteous cause in which we are engaged is not provincial, but continental. We therefore, gentlemen, shall rely upon your patriotism, abilities, firmness, and integrity to propose, join, and concur in all such measures as you shall think calculated for the common good, and to oppose such as shall appear destructive."

With the exception of an interval in 1779, when he filled the gubernatorial chair of Georgia, Mr. Walton was continued as a member of the Continental Congress until October, 1781. In association with Button Gwinnett and Lyman Hall he affixed his signature to the Declaration of Independence. As a member of the Treasury Board, of the Committee on Naval Affairs, and of other committees, he rendered intelligent and willing service. With Robert Morris and George Clymer he was commissioned to transact such continental business as might be fouud necessary to be done in Philadelphia; and George Taylor and himself were appointed commissioners to make presents to, and confer with, the Indians at Easton, Pennsylvania. It was upon his motion, in 1780, that the Treasury Board was empowered to draw bills of exchange, aggregating $100,000 in specie, at ninety days, upon the Honorable Benjamin Franklin, Minister Plenipotentiary of the United States near the court of Versailles.

With Edward Telfair and Edward Langworthy, on the 9th of July, 1778, he signed the Articles of Confederation; and on the 17th of the following December he and Dr. Lyman Hall, as special commissioners from Georgia, waited upon General Lincoln at Charlestown "to inform him of the true situation of matters in this State, and show how essentially requisite it was that some vigorous and decisive measures should be taken for its defense against the incursions of its southern neighbors."

When Colonel Campbell, late in December, 1778, effected a landing at Girardeau's Bluff and moved upon Savannah, defended by General Robert Howe, George Walton, — who then held the rank of Colonel [1] of the First Battalion of the First Regiment of Foot Militia formed for the defense of Georgia, — with one hundred men, was posted on the South Common, on the right of the American line, to guard the road leading to Great Ogeechee Ferry. Although informed by Colonel Walton that there was a private way through the swamp, by means of which the enemy could pass from the high grounds of Brewton Hill plantation and

[1] This commission was issued by the Honorable Archibald Bulloch, then Governor of Georgia, and bears date January 9, 1777.

gain the rear of the American right, and although urged by him to have that route properly observed, General Howe neglected to give the matter any attention. The consequence was that Sir James Baird, with the Light Infantry, — supported by the New York Volunteers under Colonel Trumbull, — conducted by a negro guide, following this unguarded route, gained the rear of the American right, and, falling heavily upon the militia detachment commanded by Colonel Walton, dispersed it with great loss. In this shock, Colonel Walton, severely wounded in the thigh, fell from his horse and was captured.

At the sound of these guns, Colonel Campbell, running his field pieces to the front, opened fire upon the brigades of Huger and Elbert, and ordered a vigorous charge all along his line. Attacked in front and rear, General Howe's forces gave way. A retreat was sounded; a panic ensued; and the Americans, retreating in a disorderly manner through Savannah, made their way, as best they could, to the high ground beyond the Springfield plantation swamp, leaving the town and all that it contained open to the victor.

By the musket-ball which he received while endeavoring with his militia to stay the onset of Sir James Baird, Colonel Walton's thigh was broken. Judge T. U. P. Charlton says that he never recovered from the effect of this wound, but limped to the day of his death.

The following letter (the original of which lies before us), penned with a trembling hand from his couch of pain, and addressed to his young wife, will be read with interest: —

"SAVANNAH, 4 *January*, 1779, 11 o'clock, P. M.

"MY DEAR GIRL, — I was very happy to hear just this moment, by a flag, that you were safely arrived in Carolina. It is my earnest desire that you keep with your sister until you hear from me again. Your dear mamma continues still extremely ill at our house, and I am afraid that she cannot long survive.

"The day you left your brother and myself, my dear Dolly, in the chances of it I received a wound in the thigh. The bone is broke, but cures of this kind are quite common. I have every possible comfort from my conquerors, — their hospital surgeons to attend me, with Trail, Irvine, and Brydie. And they tell me they expect to see me do well. Be therefore of good spirits; and let me not hear by every flag that you are inconsolable, which will only operate to depress mine. At any rate, you ought to recollect that in these troublesome times you have no right to expect a life of superior tranquillity to your neighbors.

"My love to Polly. Brisbane is in town, perfectly well. I suppose he writes by this flag, tho' I know nothing about it, having just been apprised of it myself.

"God bless you, my dear, and remember that you are sincerely loved by a man who wishes to make honor and reputation the rule of all his actions.

"GEO. WALTON."

We reproduce also the following letter from General Howe, expressive of his sympathy with the wounded officer, and commending him for his gallant conduct on this unfortunate occasion: —

"Decr 30, 1778.

"My heart bled for your distress, my dear Walton, when I saw you yesterday. The fortitude with which you bore it is worthy of yourself. I express to you the high approbation I have of your conduct thro' the whole military procedure since this alarm happened, and in particular in the affair of yesterday, of which I can never speak but with applause without acting contrary to the dictates of my heart. Keep up your spirits. Inform me how you are, and be assured that I am, dear sir, with great regard,

"Sincerely yours, &c.,

"ROBERT HOWE.

"P. S. I dare say you will be permitted to write to me; and if you are able, pray do. Is there anything in which I can serve you?

"COLONEL WALTON."

When so far recovered from his hurt as to be able to walk, Colonel Walton was allowed to proceed to Sunbury, where for some time he remained a prisoner of war. In consideration of the fact that he was a member of the Continental Congress, that he had signed the Declaration of Independence, and that he was a prominent citizen, the British authorities at first demanded in exchange an officer with the rank of brigadier-general. His term of service in the Continental Congress having expired, he was finally exchanged for a captain in the navy, and proceeded to Augusta, which was then the capital of republican Georgia.

By the General Assembly which convened in that town in November, 1779, Colonel Walton was elected Governor of the infant Commonwealth. There were then two Executive Councils actually organized and claiming to exercise important functions within the limits of the State wasted by a common enemy and rent by internal feuds. Violent were the collisions of parties, and confused was the administration of public affairs. Southern Georgia was in the hands of the enemy, and the republican government of the upper portion of the State was impecunious, weak, and peripatetic. Fortunately, little necessity existed for the office either of legislator or of governor.

During his term of service an episode occurred which, in view of the past life of Governor Walton, appeared very strange, and militated against his veracity and fair dealing. To this day no satisfactory explanation has been offered. His friendship for Button Gwinnett, and his disappointment both at the result of the political contest with Treutlen and the unfortunate issue of the duel with McIntosh, while affording ground for strong enmity towards the General, suggest no justification of the means used to undermine his influence and compass his overthrow.

It will be remembered that in consequence of his disagreement and duel with Gwinnett, and the deplorable want of accord between the civil and military authorities in Georgia in 1777, General McIntosh had been induced to quit his service at home and seek employment in some other quarter. Returning after an absence of more than two years, during the siege of Savannah and in the bloody assault by the allied army upon the British works around that town on the morning of the 9th of October, 1779, he had given fresh proof of his courage, and of his devotion to State and nation. While absent from Georgia he received a letter from George Walton, in which, commenting upon the unfortunate condition of affairs, he said: "The demon Discord yet presides in this country, and God only knows when his reign will be at an end. I have strove so hard to do good with so poor a return, that, were the liberties of America secure, I would bid adieu to all public employment, to politics, and to strife; for even virtue itself will meet with enmity."

It was General McIntosh's hope that time had healed all wounds, and that, without reproach, he would be permitted to devote his energies and military talents to the defense of Georgia. In this expectation he was mistaken. On the 30th of November, 1779, a letter purporting to be signed by William Glascock, Speaker of the Georgia House of Representatives, was transmitted to the President of the Continental Congress by George Walton, Governor of Georgia. Congress was therein assured of the dissatisfaction of the people of Georgia at the assignment of General McIntosh to the command of the military forces in that State. It was earnestly recommended that the national assembly would, while he remained in commission, indicate "some distant field for the exercise of his abilities." So thoroughly did this communication — supplemented by the representations of General McIntosh's enemies — poison the minds of the members of that body that on the 15th of February, 1780, they voted to "dispense with the services of Brigadier-General McIntosh until the further order of Congress."

Informed of this correspondence, General McIntosh promptly demanded an explanation from its alleged author. Mr. Glascock at once denied the authenticity of the document, and, on the 12th of May, 1780, addressed a letter to the President of Congress in which he denounced the communication of November, 1779, as a "flagrant forgery," and disclaimed both knowledge and paternity of it. He added: "I am glad of the opportunity of informing Congress that so far is that forgery from truth, that I believe there is not a respectable citizen or officer in Georgia who would not be happy in serving under General McIntosh; nor one in either class who would be otherwise except a few who are governed by design or self-interest." Mr. Glascock also furnished General McIntosh with a copy of this communication.

Strange as it may appear, an examination into the matter disclosed the fact that the letter to which the name of the Speaker of the House of Representatives was forged had been suggested, dictated, and forwarded by Governor Walton and certain members of his Council, with the design of impairing the influence of General McIntosh and compassing his removal from military command in Georgia. Whether Governor Walton was personally cognizant of the forgery, or whether he was deceived and imposed upon by members of his Council who were individually responsible for the malevolent act, must remain in doubt. In any event, he was instrumental in promoting a nefarious scheme, which, fortunately, failed to accomplish the unlawful result at which it aimed. So far from injuring the popularity and usefulness of the meritorious officer whose valuable services were called in question, it drew down upon its authors the condemnation of all fair-minded people.

Upon the termination of the Revolutionary War, this whole affair formed a subject of inquiry and review by the Georgia Legislature. On the journal of the House of Assembly, under date of January 30, 1783, appear the following resolutions: —

"Resolved, that they have examined such papers and persons as have been offered by the different parties, from which it appears that the resolves of Council, dated at Augusta, December 12, 1779, and the letter from Governor Walton to the President of Congress, dated December 15, 1779, respecting General McIntosh, were unjust, illiberal, and a misrepresentation of facts; that the letter said to be from William Glascock, Speaker of the Assembly, dated November 30, 1779, addressed to the President of Congress, appears to be a forgery, in violation of law and truth, and highly injurious to the interest of the State, and dangerous to the rights of its citizens; and that the Attorney-General be ordered to make the necessary inquiries, and enter such prosecutions as may be consistent with his duty and office.

"Resolved, that General McIntosh be informed that this House does entertain an abhorrence of all such injurious attempts made use of, as appears by the papers laid before them, to injure the character of an officer and a citizen of this State who merits the attention of the Legislature for his early, decided, and persevering efforts in the defense of America, of which virtue this House has the highest sense."

It is a curious fact that the very day before the adoption of these resolutions the Legislature had elected George Walton Chief Justice of the State of Georgia; thus practically rendering impossible any prosecution so far as he was concerned, and intimating that he, at least, was not personally responsible for the forgery, however much he may have been instrumental in endorsing and bringing it to the notice of the Continental Congress.

Short and uneventful was the gubernatorial career of Mr. Walton in 1779. By the ensuing General Assembly Richard Howley was, on the 4th of January, 1780, elected Governor, and Edward Telfair, George Walton, Benjamin Andrew, Lyman Hall, and William Few were appointed Delegates to the Continental Congress.

While members of and in attendance upon this Congress, Messrs. Walton, Few, and Howley apprehended that it was the design of the British ministry to submit overtures of peace upon the basis of freedom to such portions of America as were then in the possession of the Revolutionists, and of retention by the Crown of such other parts as were actually held by the King's forces. As Georgia at that time was largely under the dominion of the enemy, deeming it their duty promptly and emphatically to protest against acquiescence by the Continental Congress in any such proposition, they prepared and caused to be printed in Philadelphia, in January, 1781, over their own signatures, a pamphlet entitled "Observations upon the Effects of certain late Political Suggestions, by the Delegates of Georgia." Referring to the fact that Georgia had been in great measure reduced by conquest, they entered forcible plea against the entertainment of the doctrine of *uti possidetis*, and urged that inasmuch as the inhabitants of that Province had united in the common cause, and had expended their blood and fortunes in its support, "it would be unjust and inhuman for the other parts of the Union separately to embrace the result of the common efforts, and leavə them under the yoke of a bankrupt and enraged tyrant." "To preserve the States entire is the object of the alliance with France, and it cannot be the interest of the other great branch of the family compact that we should again make a part of the British Empire. . . . Georgia is a material part of the Union, and cannot be given up without affecting its essential interest, if not endangering its existence. . . . As to America, no part of it could expect to be long free while England retains both ends of the continent."

Whatever may have been the effect of this political tract, certain it is that, if memorialized on the subject, the Continental Congress declined to entertain the rumored basis of pacification. With the authorship of this manly protest the pen of Mr. Walton is credited.

In January, 1783, that sterling patriot and worthy gentleman, Dr. Lyman Hall, was chosen Governor of Georgia, and on the 31st of that month the Honorable George Walton was elected to fill the position of Chief Justice, with Samuel Stirk as Attorney-General. Georgia was then divided into eight counties, viz.: Wilkes, Richmond, Burke, Effingham, Chatham, Liberty, Glynn, and Camden. In each county there were two Associate Justices, and it was the duty of the Chief Justice to ride the circuit of all the counties. These journeys, as they were necessarily performed in stagecoach, private conveyance, or on horseback, were tedious and fatiguing. As illustrative of Chief Justice Walton's charges to the grand juries, we select the following, delivered in Liberty County: —

"Gentlemen of the Grand Jury, — The order and decorum with which the business of the last circuit was done in this county did not fail in producing the most general satisfaction, besides affording a happy presage of the best efforts in future from regular courts of justice. And I have now the satisfaction to inform you that an ardent desire for a strict execution of the laws is prevalent throughout the State.

"The late amazing augmentation of the number of our inhabitants in the Western District will soon give a new feature to our political affairs, — a consideration which ought to command the earliest attention of our elder citizens. In dispensing advantages, the mode should be our own. The settlement of the two new counties will be extremely advantageous, both on account of the addition to our national strength and the increase of agriculture. The productions of the lands bordering upon the waters of the Alatamaha must, for a considerable time, centre in Sunbury; the rebuilding, extension, and improvement of which form an object well worthy your attention. It has been devoted to suffer by the tempest and at the hands of our late cruel enemy; however, Union, Industry, and Perseverance will soon recover it. But while we contemplate these things, we should examine whether our happiness is secured upon a lasting foundation.

"The number of the inhabitants which conducted the late contest, both in the cabinet and the field, to its glorious issue will soon be inferior to that which will be made up of new residents. Is it not, therefore, prudent to consider whether the Constitution — the present basis of our laws — was calculated in the prospect of such an event? And whether it would not be wise to model the necessary improvements while in our power? The sacrifices we have made for the establishment of the liberties of this country should neither be forgotten nor their rewards relinquished. The people in the counties lying on Savannah River are promoting petitions for that end, and I submit the example to your discretion and judgment.

"There is one thing, gentlemen, that I cannot forbear to mention to you in particular, and that is the extreme inconvenient periods pointed out for holding your courts. To go through the labour of riding and attending five successive courts, at the distance of two hundred miles from the capital, and then to post down forty miles further to Liberty County, is distressing indeed, and too much to be punctually performed. I would fain hope, therefore, that the people of this county will promote the passing of an act authorizing the next circuit to begin instead of ending here, which will enable the law officers with more ease and certainty to perform their duty, and will afford time for the trial of appeals which now are or may be made merely for a delay of justice.

"Gentlemen, I have heard of no material infractions of the law since the last session. If there have been any, the magistrates will furnish the Attorney-General with the necessary informations, and they shall be duly attended to. Your local evils, if you have any, you will please to make known to the public by presentment. GEO. WALTON.

"SUNBURY, 13 April, 1784."

In 1787 Judge Walton was appointed a Delegate from the State of Georgia to the Federal Convention charged with revising the Articles of Confederation, and reporting such alterations and provisions as might be deemed adequate to the emergencies of government and the preservation of the Union. Prevented by judicial engagements, he did not attend. The year previous he had represented Georgia in the preliminary settlement of differences touching the boundary line between that State and South Carolina.

In 1789 he occupied for a second time the gubernatorial chair. The term of service then lasted for only one year. It was during his administration that Georgia remodeled her Constitution. Augusta was still the capital of the State, and it was here that Governor Walton received from the President of the Constitutional Convention the Constitution then adopted, affixed the seal of state to it, and proclaimed its provisions for the information of the inhabitants. As indicating the paucity of the population at that time, the following printed copies of the newly adopted Constitution were deemed sufficient for public needs and general information in the several counties then comprised within the limits of Georgia: "Ordered, that copies of the Constitution be distributed as follows:— To Camden County, 26 copies; to Glynn County, 26 copies; to Liberty County, 52 copies; to Chatham County, 70 copies; to Effingham County, 26 copies; to Burke County, 52 copies; to Richmond County, 52 copies; to Wilkes County, 70 copies; to Washington County, 26 copies; to Greene County, 26 copies; and to Franklin County, 26 copies."

With the pacification of the Creek Indians, and with the protection of the frontiers of Georgia against their depredations, Governor Walton was largely employed.

Upon the occasion of President Washington's visit to Augusta in 1791, Judge Walton was Chairman of the Reception Committee, and on behalf of the citizens prepared and presented the Address of Welcome. It was couched in the following complimentary terms: —

"To the President of the United States of America:

"Sir, — Your journey to the Southward being extended to the frontier of the Union, affords a fresh proof of your indefatigable zeal in the service of your country, and equal attention and regard to all the people of the United States. With these impressions, the citizens of Augusta present their congratulations upon your arrival here in health, with the assurance that it will be their greatest pleasure, during your stay with them, to testify the sincere affection they have for your person, their sense of obligation for your merits and for your services, and their entire confidence in you as the Chief Magistrate of their country. On your return, and at all times, their best wishes will accompany you, while they maintain the hope that a life of virtue, benevolence, and patriotism may be long preserved for the benefit of the age and the example of posterity."

To this address the President was pleased to return the following answer: —

"Gentlemen, — I receive your congratulations on my arrival in Augusta with great pleasure. I am much obliged by your assurances of regard, and thank you with unfeigned sincerity for the favorable sentiments you are pleased to express towards me.

"Entreating you to be persuaded of my gratitude, I desire to assure you that it will afford me the most sensible satisfaction to learn the progression of your prosperity. My best wishes for your happiness, collectively and individually, are sincerely offered."

In 1795 and 1796 Mr. Walton represented Georgia as a Senator in the Congress of the United States. He was a member of the Union Society of Savannah, and a trustee of the Richmond Academy. As one of the first trustees of the University of Georgia, he rendered valuable service in formulating plans and adopting measures for the promotion of higher education in Georgia.

For many years, and at the time of his death, he was Judge of the Middle Circuit of this Commonwealth. The State was then divided into three judicial districts, — the Eastern, the Middle, and the Western. The Middle Circuit embraced the following counties: Screven, Burke, Montgomery, Washington, Warren, Richmond, Columbia, and Jefferson. As a judge, few men in this Commonwealth ever attained unto, and none transcended, the reputation acquired and maintained by Mr. Walton.

Upon the conclusion of peace he established his home near Augusta, and there resided until the day of his death, spending his winters upon his farm, called "Meadow Garden,"[1] then on the outskirts of the town, and now within the corporate limits of the city, and his summers on Mount Salubrity, afterwards known as the Sand Hills, and at present within the confines of the village of Summerville.

[1] The dwelling-house still stands.

During the night of the 2d of February, 1804, Judge Walton died suddenly at his winter residence, Meadow Garden. For many years he had been a martyr to the gout. The death of his eldest son, just entering upon manhood, well educated, amiable, and full of promise, exerted a depressing influence, and is thought to have hastened the demise of his distinguished father. Upon the announcement of his dissolution the community was profoundly impressed, and united in paying the most marked funeral honors. The members of the Richmond Bar convened at once, passed complimentary resolutions, and arrayed themselves in mourning. Upon the day appointed for the funeral a procession, consisting of

"The City Marshal,
The Intendant,
Members of the City Council,
The Sheriff of the County of Richmond,
The Governor of Georgia and his Aids,
The Secretaries of Departments and Clerks,
Magistrates and other Public Officers,
Attendant Physician and Clergymen,
The Corpse,
The Pall-bearers,
The Chief Mourners,
Members of the Bar,
Trustees of the Richmond Academy,
Rector, Assistants, and Pupils,
Citizens walking two and two,
The Company of Rangers, and
The Artillery firing Minute Guns,"

moved from Meadow Garden through the streets of Augusta and to the family cemetery of Colonel Robert Watkins at Rosney, where the remains of the honored dead were interred. Nothing was omitted which could lend dignity and solemnity to the demonstration, or evidence the general sorrow at the departure of this illustrious citizen. Here the bones of Judge Walton rested until their removal in 1848, when, in association with those of the Honorable Lyman Hall, they were inhumed beneath the monument in Greene Street, in front of the Court House, in Augusta, Georgia, erected by patriotic hands in memory of the Signers from this Commonwealth of the Declaration of Independence. The corner stone was laid on the 4th of July in that year by the Masonic Fraternity with appropriate rites. Eloquent addresses were delivered by the Honorable William C. Dawson and by William T. Gould, Esquire.

The purpose was to locate beneath this monument the bones of all the Signers from Georgia, but the grave of Button Gwinnett, — who received his mortal hurt in the duel with General Lachlan McIntosh in 1777, — although believed to be in the old cemetery on South Broad Street, in Savannah, being without a stone could not be identified. The remains of Dr. Lyman Hall were readily obtained from the brick vault on his plantation near Shell Bluff, in Burke County. Parties were still in life who could point out the grave of Governor Walton in the Rosney cemetery, although unmarked by a monument, and in removing his bones the trace of the ball which shattered his thigh in 1778 was still apparent in the osseous structure, and in the effort which nature had made to repair the injury then sustained. Dr. I. P. Garvin, Mayor, and Councilmen Dr. L. A. Dugas, Benjamin Conley, and G. F. Parish constituted the committee from the City Council of Augusta charged with the collection of the bones of the Signers, their reinterment, and the erection of the memorial shaft above them.

After describing the events which rendered the observance of the 4th of July, 1848, memorable in the history of Augusta, the editor of "The Constitutionalist" newspaper concludes with these patriotic sentiments: —

"We cannot close this notice without alluding to the interesting fact that the honored dust of two of the Signers of the Declaration of Independence, born in distant sections of the Union, now repose harmoniously together under the stone which marks a spot in our city forever sacred and hallowed.

"Let it speak a monitory voice amidst the fiercest strifes of party, and in the rising heats of sectional animosities which so fearfully threaten the destruction of the good work those immortal patriots so nobly planned. Let it act like a talisman to still the boiling passions and to quiet the blind rage of party.

"Lyman Hall was from the land of the Pilgrim Fathers. He was a native of Connecticut. He made his home upon Georgia soil, and proved himself a useful and patriotic citizen. His adopted State ever delighted to honor him while living, and gratefully embalms his memory.

"George Walton also came from another Colony to Georgia while she was yet struggling in her infancy. He was a native of the Old Dominion, — of Frederick County, Virginia. Thus does it seem that in the days that tried men's souls there were patriots from every section of the Old Union, one in principle, one in feeling, though various skies smiled on their birth; and, as a band of brothers, they wrought out for us a heritage of Freedom for which we owe them a common debt of gratitude."

It is rather a singular fact that Judge Walton, who for so many years recognized the expediency of wills and administered the laws appertaining to them, died intestate. Upon her application, submitted on the 2d of April, 1804, administration upon his estate was granted to his widow, her bond being fixed at the sum of twenty-five thousand dollars.

Alluding to the services rendered and the honors won by Judge Walton, the author of the sketch in Sanderson's "Biography of the Signers to the Declaration of Independence" says: "There are indeed few men in the United States upon whom more extensive and solid proofs of public confidence have been lavished. He was six times elected a Representative to Congress, twice Governor of the State, once a Senator of the United States, and four times Judge of the Superior Courts; the latter office he held during fifteen years and until the day of his death. He was one of the Commissioners on the part of the United States to negotiate a treaty with the Cherokee Indians in Tennessee, and several times a member of the State Legislature." He should have added that he was also Chief Justice of Georgia.

In every station he was capable and conscientious, observant of the trust reposed, and conspicuous in the careful discharge of the appurtenant duties. As an officer of the militia he was prompt and energetic, displaying great gallantry in the presence of the enemy. As a citizen he was alert, public-spirited, firm in his convictions, and courageous in the advocacy of right and liberty. Warm in his attachments, he did not hesitate to avow his enmities.

Indulging in no temporizing policy, he was manly

and open in his affiliations and in his dislikes. Stern in his conceptions of right and duty, he was by nature aristocratic in his sentiments, and pandered not to the whims of the *vulgus commune.* In no degree was he either a time-server or a suppliant for popular favor. Merit he recognized and encouraged. Learning and talent he held in special esteem. Of quick temper, and entertaining a nice conception of the proprieties of the occasion, he insisted upon a strict observance of the respect due to station, and suffered neither neglect nor slight at the hands of subordinates. In conversation he was terse, being partial to short and comprehensive expressions. Satire he often employed with marked effect.

Generous in his mode of living, much given to study, and neglectful of regular exercise, before he attained unto middle life he became subject to attacks of gout which grew more frequent and violent as he advanced in years, engendering much suffering, and in the end proving the cause of his death. He often remarked to his physician that an entertaining volume was the most effectual remedy for this malady. Of the society of students and the well informed he was fond, and it was his delight to lead youthful minds in the paths of knowledge; or, as he expressed it, "to put the young beagles upon the track in the chase."

Among those who pursued their legal studies under his immediate counsel and instruction may be mentioned the Honorable James Jackson, afterwards United States Senator from and Governor of Georgia.[1]

Seldom exempt from the claims of public affairs, he evinced little desire for the accumulation of wealth.

[1] T. U. P. Charlton's *Life of Major-General James Jackson*, p. 49. Augusta, Georgia, 1809.

His salary, supplemented by a small income from his farm, sufficed for the comfortable maintenance of himself and family. When not engaged in the discharge of official duties he spent most of his time in his study. His books were his constant and his favorite companions. "Come, my best friends, my books, and lead me on," seemed his ever-recurring salutation. His early thirst for knowledge remained unabated until the end of his life.

Only one son — George Walton, commissioned Second Lieutenant in the Second Regiment of Light Artillery in May, 1808 — survived him. While a resident of Pensacola he received, on the 17th of May, 1822, from Andrew Jackson, the appointment of "Secretary in and for the Territory of East Florida." He subsequently removed to Mobile, Alabama. He was the father of Octavia Walton, who, as Madame Le Vert, attained prominence in the social and literary world.

Comely in person, dignified and reserved in his manners, Judge Walton was a marked personage in any assembly. Of his features excellent memory has been preserved by a miniature painted by the elder Peale, now treasured by the Signer's great-great-grandson, Master George Walton Reab, of Summerville, near Augusta, Georgia. It was from this likeness that the engraved portrait was made which forms one of the illustrations of the writer's second volume of the "History of Georgia."

This Commonwealth has named one of her counties in honor of this patriot, who, as soldier, statesman, judge, legislator, senator, governor, and signer, rendered service varied and most valuable, leaving an impress upon his age and generation which has suffered no oblivion at the hands of intervening years.

JOHN WALTON.

WITH regard to this member of the old Congress we have been able to gather but little information. A brother of the Honorable George Walton, he was born in Virginia about 1738. To the Provincial Congress which assembled at Savannah on the 4th of July, 1775, he was a Delegate representing the Parish of St. Paul. On the 20th of July of the previous year, in association with Noble W. Jones, Archibald Bulloch, and John Houstoun, he signed the public call which convoked the liberty-loving citizens of Georgia, under the eye and in defiance of the protest of the Royal Governor. Of the Executive Council, chosen when John Adam Treutlen was elected first Republican Governor, he was a member. By the General Assembly of Georgia Mr. Walton was, on the 26th of February, 1778, commissioned as a Delegate to the Continental Congress.

His home was then at New Savannah, situated in the county of Richmond, on the Savannah River, not many miles below the town of Augusta. Here he owned and cultivated a plantation, the principal market crop of which was indigo. As we write, one of his letters lies before us, written from this place, dated on the 21st of January, 1777, and addressed to the Honorable Edward Telfair. In this communication Mr. Walton advises that gentleman of a shipment of indigo he had recently made to him, and bespeaks his best efforts in effecting advantageous sale of the consignment.

For a number of years Mr. Walton held the office of Surveyor of Richmond County. He died at New Savannah in 1783. His will is now of file in the Ordinary's Office in Augusta. It is dated the 11th of June, 1778, and was admitted to probate on the 24th of June, 1783. George Walton, William Glascock, and Britton Dawson were named as executors. He left a considerable estate, consisting of lands and negroes. The maiden name of his wife was Elizabeth Claiborne. Several children were born of this marriage, and their descendants may be found in Georgia to the present day.

JOSEPH WOOD.

He is said to have been a Pennsylvanian by birth. In 1774 he was a resident of the town of Sunbury, in the Parish of St. John and State of Georgia. Repudiating the conclusions of the Provincial meeting of the 10th of August, 1774, which, although patriotic in their character, did not culminate in placing Georgia in full affiliation with her twelve sisters and in commissioning Delegates to the Continental Congress, the inhabitants of the Parish of St. John resolved to act independently and in advance of the rest of the Colony. On the 9th of February, Joseph Wood, Daniel Roberts, and Samuel Stevens — members of the Parish committee — were deputed with a carefully prepared letter to repair to Charlestown and request of the Committee of Correspondence their "permission to form an alliance with them, and to conduct trade and commerce according to the act of non-importation to which they had already acceded."

Reaching Charlestown on the 23d of February, Messrs. Wood, Roberts, and Stevens waited upon the General Committee and earnestly endeavored to accomplish their mission. While admiring the patriotism of the Parish, and entreating its citizens to persevere in their laudable exertions, the Carolinians, deeming it "a violation of the Continental Association to remove the prohibition in favor of any *part* of a Province," declined the application.

Nothing daunted, the inhabitants of St. John's Parish "resolved to prosecute their claims to an equality with the Confederated Colonies," and commissioned Dr. Lyman Hall to represent them in the Continental Congress. Returning to Pennsylvania during the early portion of the Revolutionary War, Mr. Wood entered the Continental service with the Second Pennsylvania Regiment. His promotion was rapid. He was advanced to a Majority on the 4th of January, 1776, to a Lieutenant-Colonelcy on the 29th of July in the same year, and to a full Colonelcy on the 7th of September, 1776.

Toward the close of that year, Colonel Wood was again in Georgia, where he was cordially welcomed. In January, 1777, he was elected a Delegate from Georgia to the Continental Congress, and this compliment was repeated in February of the following year.

His plantation was on North New Port River, not far from the village of Riceboro, in Liberty County (formerly St. John's Parish). The tradition of Colonel Wood's unblemished life and manly virtues still lingers in the community. Joseph Wood departed this life at his plantation in Liberty County, Georgia, in 1791. His will was probated on the 2d of October in that year. His widow, Catholina, two sons, John and Jacob, and two daughters, Hester and Elizabeth, are therein named as legatees and devisees.

JOHN JOACHIM ZUBLY.

A NATIVE of St. Gall, Switzerland, where he was born on the 27th of August, 1724, Mr. Zubly was engaged in the discharge of clerical duties at Wando Neck, in the Province of South Carolina, when, on the 25th of April, 1758, he received and accepted a call to a large and influential Presbyterian congregation in Savannah, Georgia. It was not, however, until 1760 that he entered fully upon his pastoral charge of that Independent Presbyterian Church. He was a clergyman of marked ability, eloquence, and learning; preaching with equal ease and power in the German, French, and English languages. A rigid disciple of Calvin, he was tireless in the discharge of his professional labors. Under his guidance, his congregation became the most numerous and popular within the limits of Georgia. In 1770 he was complimented by Princeton College with the degree of Doctor of Divinity.

By an act of the Colonial Legislature, approved on the 17th of March, 1758, Georgia was divided into Parishes, and the patronage of the Crown was specially extended in aid of churches professing the Episcopal faith. While not favored by exclusive recognition, the purpose appeared to be to accord to that denomination, within the limits of Georgia, a prestige akin to that which the Church of England enjoyed within the realm; to create certain offices and provide emoluments for the encouragement of that religious persuasion, and the extension of the gospel in accordance with its forms of worship and mode of government; and to prescribe a method by which faithful registers of births, marriages, christenings, and deaths might be kept and perpetuated. Numerous were the Dissenters then in the Province. They were represented by Presbyterians, Lutherans, Congregationalists, Methodists, a few Baptists, and some Hebrews. To all sects save Papists was free toleration accorded; and whenever a Dissenting congregation organized and applied for a grant of land whereon to build a church, the petition did not pass unheeded. There can be no doubt, however, that it was the intention of the Government, both Royal and Colonial, to engraft the Church of England upon the Province, and, within certain limits, to advance its prosperity and insure its permanency. At the same time an adherence to its rubrics was in no wise made a condition precedent to political preferment.

Despite the advantage thus enjoyed by the Episcopal Church, so popular was Mr. Zubly as a preacher, and so acceptable were his ministrations, that he soon attracted many of the leading citizens of Savannah. So catholic were his views, so pronounced was the interest which he exhibited in public affairs, and so manifest were his sympathies with the protestants against the arbitrary acts of Parliament that his influence as a citizen and a lover of liberty was felt beyond the limits of his pulpit and congregation. As a compliment to the man, and to the position which he then occupied, he was elected a Delegate to the Provincial Congress which assembled in Savannah on the 4th of July, 1775. Before and at the opening of that Congress, he delivered a sermon on American affairs, entitled "The Law of Liberty," which may be accepted as a fair specimen of the composition and manly thought of this eloquent and accomplished divine. When printed by Henry Miller, of Philadelphia, it was prefaced by a forcible and conclusive plea for the liberties of America, embodied in a communication addressed by Mr. Zubly to the Right Honorable the Earl of Dartmouth.

By this Congress Dr. Zubly, in association with John Houstoun, Archibald Bulloch, Noble W. Jones, and Dr. Lyman Hall, was chosen to represent the Province of Georgia in the Continental Congress. Upon a suggestion from him that he was greatly surprised at being selected as a Delegate, and that he could not accept the honor without the consent of his congregation, Messrs. Noble W. Jones and John Houstoun were appointed a committee to interview the members of Dr. Zubly's church and request their permission that he absent himself from his charge for a season, in order that he might perform the important duties devolved upon him by the Congress. Four days afterwards those gentlemen reported that they had conferred with the congregation, and that the members expressed a willingness "to spare their minister for a time for the good of the common cause." Dr. Zubly thereupon declared his acceptance of the appointment, and thanked the Congress for this mark of honor and confidence.

By this Congress the Reverend Doctor Zubly was placed upon four important committees, — one to prepare a petition to the King "upon the present unhappy situation of affairs;" another to address a letter to the President of the Continental Congress, acquainting him fully with the proceedings of this Provincial

Congress; a third to frame an address to His Excellency Governor Wright; and a fourth to constitute a Committee of Intelligence.

From the addresses then prepared we reproduce the following: —

"To the Inhabitants of the Province of Georgia:

"Fellow-Countrymen, — We are directed to transmit to you an account of the present state of American affairs, as well as the proceedings of the late Provincial Congress.

"It is with great sorrow we are to acquaint you that what our fears suggested, but our reason thought impossible, is actually come to pass.

"A civil war in America is begun. Several engagements have already happened. The friends and foes of America have been equally disappointed. The friends of America were in hopes British troops could never be induced to slay their brethren. It is, however, done, and the circumstances are such as must be an everlasting blot on their character for humanity and generosity. An unfeeling commander has found means to inspire his troops with the same evil spirit that possesseth himself. After the starving, helpless, innocent inhabitants of Boston delivered up their arms and received his promise that they might leave that virtuous, devoted town, he is said to have broke his word; and the wretched inhabitants are still kept to fall a prey to disease, famine, and confinement. If there are powers which abhor injustice and oppression, it may be hoped such perfidy cannot go long unpunished.

"But the enemies of America have been no less disappointed. Nothing was so contemptible in their eyes as the rabble of an American militia; nothing more improbable than that they would dare to look regulars in the face, or stand a single fire. By this time they must have felt how much they were mistaken. In every engagement the Americans appeared with a bravery worthy of men that fight for the liberties of their oppressed country. Their success has been remarkable; the number of the slain and wounded on every occasion vastly exceeded theirs; and the advantages they gained are the more honourable because, with a patience that scarce has an example, they bore every act of injustice and insult till their lives were attacked, and then gave the fullest proof that the man of calmness and moderation in counsel is usually the most intrepid and courageous in battle.

"You will doubtless lament with us the hundreds that died in their country's cause; but does it not call for greater sorrow that thousands of British soldiers sought and found their deaths when they were active to enslave their brethren and their country? However irritating all these proceedings, yet so unnatural is this quarrel that every good man must wish and pray that it may soon cease; that the injured rights of America may be vindicated by milder means; and that no more blood may be shed, unless it be of those who fomented, and mean to make an advantage of, these unhappy divisions.

"From the proceedings of the Congress, a copy of which accompanies the present, you will be convinced that a reconciliation on honorable principles is an object which your Delegates never lost sight of. We have sent an humble and manly petition to his Majesty; addressed his representative, our Governor; provided, as far as in our power, for internal quiet and safety; and Delegates will soon attend the General Congress to assist and coöperate in any measure that shall be thought necessary for the saving of America.

"His Excellency, at our request, having appointed the 19th inst. as a Day of Humiliation, and news being afterwards received that the Continental Congress had recommended the 20th inst. to be observed as such, both days have been observed with a becoming solemnity; and we humbly hope many earnest prayers have been presented to the Father of Mercies on that day through this extensive continent, and that He has heard the cries of the destitute, and will not despise their prayers.

"You will permit us most earnestly to recommend to you a steady perseverance in the cause of Liberty, and that you will use all possible caution not to say or do anything unworthy of so glorious a cause; to promote frugality, peace, and good order; and, in the practice of every social and religious duty, patiently to wait the return of that happy day when we may quietly sit under our vine and fig-tree, and no man make us afraid."

We make no apology for presenting this address *in extenso*, because with its composition the pen of Dr. Zubly is credited, and because it shows how earnestly, at this epoch in his career, his sympathies were enlisted in behalf of American freedom.

Of the five Delegates thus selected by the Provincial Congress to represent Georgia in the Continental Congress, Messrs. Zubly, Bulloch, and Houstoun repaired to Philadelphia, and participated in the deliberations of that body, at an adjourned session held in September. Dr. Lyman Hall, who had been present at a previous meeting as a Delegate commissioned by the Parish of St. Paul, was now absent; and Dr. Noble W. Jones, than whom the "Sons of Liberty" claimed none more competent, courageous, and accomplished,—in deference to the entreaties of his aged father, Colonel Noble Jones, a faithful servant of the Crown, who, trembling upon the verge of the grave, bespoke the companionship of his distinguished and devoted son,—postponed for the while his service to the Province in this prominent capacity, that he might respond to his filial obligations.

Georgia was ably represented. From the inception of the disagreements between Great Britain and her American Colonies, Archibald Bulloch had been a firm friend to the liberties of America. No one stood higher in the respect and affection of his fellow-citizens, and for him the most pronounced honors were in store. John Houstoun, too, was among the most zealous advocates of the rights of the Colonies. Of honorable descent and liberal education, of admitted bravery and commanding influence, his memory is associated with some of the best traditions of the epoch, and of the community in which he dwelt.

Of the early labors of the Reverend Dr. Zubly in the cause of freedom, education, and religion, we may not speak except in praise. His course in the first Continental Congress which he attended was consistent and patriotic. The acceptable pastor of a large Presbyterian congregation in Savannah,—scholarly, gifted in speech, public-spirited, and of marked ability,—his voice and pen had been freely employed in the vindication of the rights of the Colonies against the encroachments of Parliament. Discussing the suggestions made in England to arm the slaves in order to reduce their masters to obedience to British rule, he wrote to the Earl of Dartmouth as follows: "Proposals publicly made by ministerial writers relative to American domestics laid the Southern Provinces under the necessity of arming themselves. A proposal to put it in the power of domestics to cut the throats of their masters can only serve to cover the proposers and abettors with everlasting infamy. The Americans have been called 'a rope of sand,' but *blood* and *sand* will make a firm cementation; and enough American blood has been already shed to cement them together into a threefold cord not easily to be broken." In the deliberations and utterances of the Provincial Congress in Savannah no member had borne a more prominent part.

When, however, at a subsequent session of the Continental Congress, he found himself confronted with a determination on the part of its members to sever the ties binding the American Colonies to the Mother Country, and to erect on these shores a separate, independent, and republican confederation, his heart failed him, and, opening a correspondence with Sir James Wright, he revealed to him the plans of Congress, and warned him of the impending rupture. His conduct and language exciting suspicion, he was watched, and one of his treasonable letters was seized. This fact was brought to the notice of Congress by Mr. Chase, of Maryland. So alarmed became Dr. Zubly that, precipitately abandoning his seat, he returned to Georgia, where, taking sides against the liberty people, he became so obnoxious that, in 1777, he was banished from Savannah, with the loss of half his estate. Taking refuge in South Carolina, he there remained until the Royal government was, in 1779, reëstablished in Southern Georgia. Then, returning to Savannah, he resumed his ministerial labors, and there abode until his death, which occurred on the 23d of July, 1781. Broken in heart and fortune, the latest years of his life involved a ceaseless struggle with misfortune. "His political defection," says Dr. Stevens, "while it did no harm to Georgia or the Colonies, brought misery upon himself and family, and tarnished a name which shone among the earlier patriots of Georgia with peculiar brightness. Savannah still bears the record of this learned man in the names of two of its streets, 'Joachim' and 'Zubly,' and one of the hamlets of the city is called 'St. Gall,' in honor of his birthplace in Switzerland."

His declaration, in his place in the Continental Congress, that "a republic was little better than a government of devils," and his subsequent desertion of his post to seek shelter under the authority of the Crown, were but the prelude to unhappiness, disgrace, and an early grave.

There was an oil portrait of this member of the Old Congress, but unfortunately, many years ago, it was accidentally destroyed by fire.